W...

Cairns for a Journey

❖ ❖ ❖ ❖ ❖ ❖ ❖ ❖ ❖ ❖ ❖ ❖

JIM COTTER

CAIRNS PUBLICATIONS

SHEFFIELD

2001

© Jim Cotter 1983, 1999, 2001

Parts of this book first appeared in
Prayer at Night and *Dazzling Darkness*

A companion volume to
Prayer at Day's Dawning and
Prayer at Night's Approaching

Cairns Publications
Dwylan, Stryd Fawr, Harlech,
Gwynedd, LL46 2YA
www.cottercairns.co.uk
office@cottercairns.co.uk

ISBN 1 870652 30 4 (hardback)
ISBN 1 870652 31 2 (paperback)

Typeset in Monotype Baskerville
by Strathmore Publishing Services, London N7

Printed by Biddles Ltd, Guildford

CONTENTS

For
Alan and Elin

FOREWORD

"You only need waymarks in a fog," said a friend. I reassured him that it feels as if my life has been lived in a 'cloud of unknowing', and I have always treasured the cairns and markers that have helped me to continue my spiritual pilgrimage.

Jim Cotter has been a personal waymark for me over the last twelve years, and his writing for longer than that. This collection reflects his own journey: his wrestling with his own humanity and sexuality, his trinitarian God, his 'brainsquall' – and even his need of a bishop! (See 4 July.) As with much of Jim's writing I have found that these cairns can be used for both personal and corporate meditation. I have already discovered my purple passages in this book, which I shall turn to regularly for the rest of my life and which I shall want to share with others.

Waymarks connects for me with the bustle and rhythms of Manchester and with the beauty and solitude of Llandecwyn in North Wales, where Jim now spends part of the year. They help to guide me through the fog in city and on mountain top.

STEPHEN LOWE

Bishop of Hulme

Manchester, February 2001

PREFACE

The river that is this book has many tributaries. The first was a wayward collection of thoughts and meditations, 'Cairns for a Journey', which made up the second part of *Prayer at Night*, a compilation that was first published in the early eighties in photocopied A5 format, with a light blue cover (400 copies, a collector's item?), and is now available as one of two companion volumes to this publication, new editions of *Prayer at Night's Approaching* and *Prayer at Day's Dawning*.

Some of those early cairns found their way into the audiotape version of *Prayer at Night*.

They were revised in 1998 and published in 1999 as a book with the title *Dazzling Darkness*. It is still in print, a modest twenty-eight items in total. The Introduction that follows this Preface is taken from that book.

The intention was that this would be the first of a number of mini-collections, but it now seems opportune to offer this book instead, a 'cairn for the day' throughout the year.

The first reason is that it neatly complements the other two books already mentioned. The second is that about a quarter of the collection has appeared

month by month as part of the mailing to sub-
scribers to the Cairns Network: since that network
is now no more, putting those cairns in this book
gives them a more permanent home (if a cairn can
be said to have a home!) and offers a memento.

However, two-thirds of this book is new. It is not
that these 'waymarks' have been recently planted –
indeed many of them go back years – but that they
are new to the public arena.

JIM COTTER

Sheffield, January 2001

INTRODUCTION

In 1983 I described some 'cairns for a journey' that I had slowly built over my then forty years, and published them as part of the second edition of *Prayer at Night* (there having been a chaotic pile of what I then called 'nuggets' in the pilot edition of 1981.)

Revisiting them more than a decade later, I found I had a stronger desire than before to build with my own stones, using other people's only if, over the years, they have been heartfelt and reached soul deep. I realized there were some that I had neglected. Did they need re-building, 're-membering' in a way that carried their energy into the future, or were they no longer needed as markers?

I found myself cleaning accumulated mould from some of the stones – and chipping away at others to reveal new facets. Always there is the tough task of digging deep into old images and sayings, pondering them afresh.

Some of the more recent cairns were built as I slowly emerged from a lengthy spell of darkness, dazed by an unexpected journey, unsure of what would be shaped from strange and unfamiliar rock – as memories surfaced with their hints of potential meaning in and through what had happened.

Every metaphor – even that of the cairn – has its limits as a bearer of truth. It is hard to visualize a moving cairn, but the more it is part of me, enfleshed, carried in miniature, as it were, within me, the less helpful is this image of a fairly hefty pyramid of stones. Perhaps I can imagine carrying a set of photographs of myself sitting atop various cairns, reminders to me of significant people and events. Or perhaps they are cairns of snowballs, such as the one Andy Goldsworthy constructed and photographed above Threlkeld in the Lake District some ten years ago – and presumably has long since disappeared.

I still wish to remember one of the cairns on Loughrigg Fell, near Ambleside – not all that far from Threlkeld, the first hill I was helped up, I suspect mostly on my father's back, as a very young boy. It stands for the early truths of my life, which every so often I still stumble against and need to contemplate again if I am to grow.

So it is that some of my cairns now mark a trail I no longer need to follow. Some I am shaping for the first time in new territory, much of it seeming uncharted waste. Some I am re-arranging. A writer reflects with T. S. Eliot that he has words only for that which he no longer wishes to say – and no words yet for the experiences being delved in the heat of the sun, or at dead of night.

Some of these waymarks are addressed to 'you'. This convention does not indicate the author speaking to the reader. It is the author being addressed by 'God', 'angel', 'friend', 'inner voice'. You, the reader, are invited to overhear, and to join in the conversation with your own pondering.

A NOTE ON TREES

How many trees have been used to publish this book? Well, only the pulp is used, which comes from the trimmings: the trunks are used for furniture. A commercially grown softwood tree produces, on average, about one-sixth of a ton of pulp. Since this book has used about one ton, it has needed the pulp of six trees to produce it. But by weight it has needed only three-quarters of one tree. So Cairns Publications is donating the wherewithal for the planting of two trees, in gratitude and recompense.

WAYMARKS

1 January

The stones of the first cairn in a sequence of meditations in *Prayer at Night* (p. 54) were about being open to the night and to the God of the night. The assumption was that the 'dark hours' have something valuable to give us and that we need not be unduly afraid.

I remembered a painting in a cottage in Langdale in the Lake District (not far from my Loughrigg Fell). A hooded stranger on horseback is emerging from the mist.

Do I expect an enemy – or at least some message of minor doom?

The stranger might be a long-lost friend. It might be a moment of recognition and wonder – we have *found* each other again, even in the darkness which has no visible signposts.

Or it may be the 'strange meeting' of Wilfrid Owen's poem, between two soldiers, with the hard dark work to be done after the moment of recognition, 'I am the enemy you killed, my friend.'

This old cairn seems to me now to have been too sunny an invitation to enter the dark. It bid me pray with open hand, not with clenched fist, but I may have to begin the journey by shaking that fist at the God of the night.

The surrender of trust may be a crucial act at some point on the journey, but not at the beginning – and not without hands lacerated by rocks.

Betrayals in the secret darkness of the past are not lightly undone.

2 January

Dig through unrelenting rock into places that appear to be death-dealing.

It is only deep below the surface that diamonds wait to be mined.

Riddle the gravel in patient search for rare gold.

Recall the oyster and the pearl.

There is hard labour, a seeming waste of time and effort, a grinding small of surface self.

Even if hope is alive, it is sparse.

Even if there is a vein of mercy in the hard stone, it is thin.

There is no other route to the riches that count.

(How do they 'count'?)

3 January

Let eye and ear be keenly attentive to *everything* that is *there*, deep within you.

It is only in that unexpected place that it is possible to receive the priceless gift of hearing your own true voice.

Only then will it be worth 'speaking out'.

4 January

To embark on any adventure, any exploration of your Everests and Antarcticas, storm-bound and through long nights, of your underground caves, dark and far from the sun, is to find yourself 'up against it'.

'Adventure' is from the Latin *ad-venire*, 'to come against'.

At times the wind howls.

At times the black silence deafens.

And you 'find' yourself 'lost'.

Keep moving gently, slowly, trustingly, through the caverns of your darkness, your hatred of yourself, internalized from stigma and misuse of power, from your lack of self-worth, or from your own desire for control.

Be steady, be courageous.

The skies *will* clear.

The light *will* pierce.

The way *will* open again.

You *will* emerge more whole.

You will become straightforward and honest in your encounters with others.

You will with ease and curiosity be glad to meet those who are very different from yourself.

You will with enjoyment and skill find fresh ways of loving and being loved.

You will become strong and passionate, compassionate and kind.

5 January

[Here is a prayer, slightly altered, by George Appleton, from his book *One Man's Prayers*, SPCK, 1967, p. 13. Once in a while an image holds for years, growing rather than diminishing in heart and soul.]

Give me a candle of the Spirit as I descend to the deep places of my being.

Show me the hidden things, the creatures of my dreams, the storehouse of forgotten memories and hurts.

Take me down to the source of my being, and tell me my nature and my name.

Give me freedom to grow anew, so that I may become that self, the seed of which you planted in me at my making.

Out of the deeps I cry to you, O God.

6 January

Stranger of the night, with whom I wrestle until the break of day, wounding me in thigh and groin, drawing from me with great reluctance my nature and my name, 'Jacob', 'Heel-clutcher', 'Deceiver' of those closest to me, surprise me with a name beyond my dreaming, 'Israel', 'God-striver', 'Prevailer' against the One with whom I struggle, face-to-face with truth and God, blessed as I limp into the dawn, flesh and blood yet holding on, ready at last for that generous embrace I have denied so long.

7 January

The frontiers of the familiar are closed to you: gardens and houses are but oases on the journey, which you need – and need to love – even if much of the cherishing is perforce left to others.

You *have* to be a pioneer, journeying to places which the rest of the world ignores, the Somme, the Auschwitz, the Hiroshimas of our time, humbly and courageously opening yourself to what others do not wish to see, both good and evil.

It *is* a wilderness: but take it to your heart and bless it.

It *is* a narrow way: but do not complain – the Way chose you, and you must be thankful.

It *is* a difficult choice: but to choose what is difficult as if it were easy, *that* is faith.

Do not retreat from the unfamiliar, nor condemn it. When a civilization turns, God may not be found at the old landmarks.

[Phrases owed to others: in lines 1, 13–14: Dag Hammarskjold, *Markings*; in lines 11–12: Max Warren; in lines 15–16: W. H. Auden, *For the Time Being*; in lines 18–19: David Jones.]

8 January

Listen to the outcast within you, the only one who can redeem you from the auction of your slavery, the only one who knows the truth that whispers to your crumbling strength, the only one whose stigmatized embrace can warm your frozen and excluding heart, who, silenced through long fear of you, has learned a wisdom that you desperately need, whom you can trust to befriend you and transform you, who will not exile or expel you, stranger though you have become.

9 January

Listen not to the fury, but to the zephyrs.
Listen not to the clamour, but to the whispers.
Listen not to the confusion, but to the heartbeat.
Listen not to the chatter, but to the silence.
Listen not to the surface discord, but to the deep
    harmonies.

10 January

Listen to the inscape of your neglected soul, where the voices of the poor and oppressed bring un-imagined gifts to your tyrant surface self (just as in the landscape of the outer world).

Listen to what you have neglected, to what has grown monstrous because unrecognized, to your pain, distress, and fear.

Fierce dragons guard rare treasure: they are your allies.

So too are those 'others' of whom you are afraid.

Ask these questions, have compassion on the other, create a place of welcome in your heart.

Are you white and afraid of black faces?

Are you washed out and afraid of rainbow people?

Are you a man and afraid of women – or a woman and afraid of men?

Are you heterosexual and afraid of your gay and lesbian neighbours?

Are you rich and afraid to walk the inner city streets?

Are you young and never even think of nursing homes?

Are you healthy and afraid of the death bed?

Are you fit and afraid of a permanent limp?

Are you smooth-skinned and alarmed at the first wrinkle in the mirror?

Are you busy and afraid of being useless?

The usual and the frequent may be the statistical norm: they are not necessarily normal.

And who are the especially favoured in your engodded eyes?

11 January

[R. M. Rilke wrote about the questions that yield no easy answers. The phrases quoted here have gone deep in me over the years. They come from his book, *Letters to a Young Poet*, © translated by M. D. Hester Norton, published by W. W. Norton, New York and London, 1934, 1954, 1962, p. 35.]

Be patient towards the unsolved.

Love the questions themselves.

Realize that answers come only when you are able to live them.

Live the questions now.

Gradually, without realizing it, in the distant future, you may come to live into the answers.

12 January

Reflect when you find yourself wanting to seize or grab a person or thing:

Do you react immediately, with no interval for pondering, because of the discomfort that grows in the waiting, the hunger, the loneliness?

Are you escaping into comfort or excitement?

It takes courage to pause, to be still, to be patient.

It takes courage to go *through* the feelings without *of necessity* acting on them.

It takes courage to lay aside habitual self-hatred and failure to accept your own worth and dignity.

It takes courage to love yourself.

It takes courage to realize that you cannot *make* yourself special, and to know that all you can do is simply to recognize that you are special.

Taste, then, but pause, and only then *decide* whether to spit or to swallow.

Only in this way do you learn to *respond* rather than to *react*, to move from a fresh discovered place of inner truth, no longer demanding, insisting, consciously or unconsciously.

Now you can *ask* for what you need, knowing that you will survive rejection or refusal, expectant that you are likely to be surprised by unpredictable gifts, again *knowing* the difference between compulsive searching and *shared* moments of comfort or excitement.

13 January

Perhaps this waiting, this pausing, this expectancy, is part of your journey into 'God', when, at moments secret or spectacular, you are aware of the Other Within, the Beyond in your Midst, the Fiery yet Companionable Mystery, at the depth of your human desiring, where there is an overlap with so much more.

Perhaps the ancient hunger and thirst for the living God is so bound up with your half-known desires, that you begin to encounter the Mystery, sometimes alone in the inscape, sometimes with others in the landscape, where you habitually trap others and are trapped by them in slaveries of different kinds, where you remain strangers wary of one another, where you are 'dis-placed' persons, out of true with self or place.

In encountering the Mystery of Universal Loving, engaging with your 'half'-hearted loving, you discover that you have been 're-placed' in truth, that you can move towards the stranger without fear, that you can join with others in the dismantling of your own chains and theirs.

❖

14 January

Aloneness is neutral.

To be alone is simply to be at a distance – in bathroom or crowded café.

Loneliness is negative.

To be lonely is to dislike being alone, even to be cramped and embittered by it.

But to be alone or to live alone is not necessarily something to dread.

For solitude is positive.

To be solitary is not to exclude or be excluded.

It is to be in touch with the springs of your own creativity.

It is to be aware that we can never be separate from anyone.

It is to know at the deepest level what it is to love and be loved.

15 January

For Rilke, human beings are struggling to shape their loving anew, that of two solitudes who protect and border (or touch) and salute (or greet) each other.

For Laurens van der Post, when a whole civilization goes through a dark night, only those who

accept the journey through the dark side of being
alone can be true companions to each other: they
are bound to be hermits, or at most hermits in
pairs.

[R. M. Rilke's words about two solitudes are from his *Letters to a
Young Poet*, translated by M. D. Hester Norton and published by
Norton, New York, 1934, 1954, 1962, p. 59.

Laurens van der Post wrote about the loneliness he came
across in so many people on his travels in his book *Jung and the
Story of Our Time*, published by the Hogarth Press, London,
1976, p. 41.]

16 January

Listen to the language of your wounds.

You cannot avoid suffering, but you may find
courage to grow through it, striving with difficulty
and failure, producing fruit that is strange and
unexpected, refusing to sink into bitterness, transforming grief into compassion.

For R. S. Shannon, the *wounded* oyster changes
grit to pearl.

For Léon Bloy, our hearts are wounded, even
broken, that something new may come to life in us.

For Charles Williams, the challenge is to live
from the depths of the wounds, to make the extent
of our desolation the extent of our realm.

17 January

We so often fear intimacy because our early intrinsic tenderness was violated, by abuse, violence, or withdrawal.

Seek then your own hurt child, often wandering in Auden's unending wastes, who waits and longs to speak to you in the language of those ancient wounds, who needs your adult caring strength in order to begin to trust again, so that the gifts may be released that have for so long been hidden away.

And when the healing is not yet complete, or when the scars are sensitive to touch, or when you limp to the end of your days, you may still be blessed, and discover you are given, like Jacob of old, your new name.

For John Collis, tensions remained from being a rejected twin, but he used the strings to make new music, playing tunes that would not otherwise have been heard.

He asks if we would deny ourselves such a high calling for the sake of ease – or even happiness?

18 January

There is a pain, a wound, a sorrow, that cannot be taken away: it can only be endured, lived through, and in the process sometimes transformed – the once in a while parable of hope.

We can in a small measure share one another's pain, indeed do all we can to diminish it. But it is a lie to pretend that it will all go away, suddenly or gradually.

More realistically, to have your wound 'touched' by hands that will hold but not intrude or harm is to know yourself alive and loved: alas that something so everyday should be a 'miracle', a source of wonder, to so many who have been maimed.

19 January

Once you know the *solidarity* of pain you can begin to mould it, to use this very raw material to shape – what?

There are no words for it, it is a – glory? – that has not yet been born.

You have this choice – to add to the world's pain by inflicting more, or by prayer and touch to lessen its power over you.

In the bearing together of our pain, not fighting

it or increasing it, but going with its grain, you discover a light that begins to penetrate the dark places, and there grows a wisdom that uses the power of the dark to create what is new in the world.

20 January

The pain of the world will not cease until all humankind, here and beyond, has come together in the love of the pain-bearers, and until that happens, the glimpses we are given of joy and healing throw into sharp relief the pain of others that never seems to yield.

Our own healing can give hope only if the scars of our wounds are visible, the pain transformed to the deep compassion of an aching loving heart.

21 January

For Milosz, prayer is the source of life, but it is the prayer that comes not from the mouth but 'from the lips of wounds'.

For Angelus Silesius,

> There is no higher aim
> than to reclaim
> another, blinded by life's pain,
> to help him see and live again.

William Blake bids us

> Seek love in the pity of another's woe,
> In the gentle relief of another's care,
> In the darkness of night and the winter's snow,
> In the naked and outcast – seek love there.

Julian of Norwich prayed that our only wounds might be these: the wound that we cannot avoid because we belong to one another, and feel and hear the murmur of the world's pain; the wound of a sense of compassion for others; the wound of a sense of longing for God.

[I have lost track of the quotation from Milosz. That from Angelus Silesius, seventeenth-century Polish poet, comes from the translation of his work by Frederick Franck, and is published as *The Book of Angelus Silesius* by Wildwood House, London, 1976.]

22 January

Love your body.

   You are a body: not a no-body, not just any-body, but some-body.

   And we are a Body, a Living Organism that some have been drawn to name as the Living Christ.

   The body is the dwelling place of the whole-making Spirit.

   You are a body in the milieu of Spirit.

23 January

God accepts you as you are.

   God is creating you as a loving, sexual, bodily being.

   God is at the heart of your striving, of your giving and receiving, drawing you closer in the energies of love, always pursuing, luring, inviting, never letting go.

24 January

Whatever your unique mix and measure of sexuality, be very glad: to be a human sexual 'is fundamental and ordinary and exceptional'.

And because you are loved unconditionally, you don't have to take yourself too seriously.

If you were the finger of God, and all the world were ticklish…

[The phrase in quotation marks comes from Iris Murdoch.]

25 January

If you have been *deeply wounded*, physically – emotionally – sexually, 'in the groin', by rejection of your sexuality, by rejection of your flesh-body, by a physical wound to the flesh, by violating intrusion, healing cannot easily occur in places of passion: the pulses of energy are so strong that they can overwhelm the vulnerable and hurting, and inloveness always has its siren strains.

Neither can healing occur if you cut off from the ache of the wound, if you refuse to visit its territory, if you compensate by the desperate search for sensation, release, excitement.

Rather does the search need to be for different moments of bodily loving and touch, in the assurance of another's steady love…small healing sacraments of touch, where loneliness is relieved, where delight is shared, where flesh is comforted, where sleep comes in the other's arms.

Deep love, gentle touch, steady goodwill: these
are the healers.

Then, deeply affirmed as good, bodies can contain the mightier passions.

Without the ground bass of the quieter moments,
the louder ones, like exploding shells, destroy or
freeze: they are blows that shock the body into a
deathly rigidity.

26 January

If the wounding is so deep that you never reach the
place where passion can be contained, you have no
other healing choice than to be loyal to the quieter
ways, *where just as much love is made.*

There are dark times when this is not believable,
when even the sustaining love of another cannot be
received, however much it is offered and yearned for.

The *experience* of love is far distant, and the temptation is to despair.

All that can be done is to cleave to hope, loyally
bearing the wounds, gently probing them, living
and delving the space between yourself and the
other...

Then, at unlooked-for moments, the touch of a
finger is enough to create a universe.

For a life-changing fragment of time, you are convinced that there *is* 'a dearest freshness deep down things'.

[Acknowlegment to Gerard Manley Hopkins for that last phrase.]

27 January

You are destined to be makers of love, passionately and tenderly, focused genitally and diffused bodily, yet always in the flesh.

For Lige Clarke and Jack Nichols, the most loving sexual act of all is gently to reach for another and through touch to make that person feel whole.

[That last thought is from Lige Clarke and Jack Nichols' book, *I Have More Fun With You Than Anybody*, published in 1972 by the St Martin's Press, New York.]

28 January

Human beings have always drawn boundaries between the clean and the dirty, but ask this:

After making love, do you feel you need a bath, or that you have had a bath?

29 January

Your regrets should be about those you have not touched, those you have neglected to say and show that you love them.

For the American novelist Merle Miller, the commandment is this: Go forth and touch… Thou shalt not commit unloving…

In such ways is the creative Spirit released in you, to take bodily shape in ways you can never entirely predict.

In such ways you live the life of God, the God who, for Sebastian Moore, is an intimacy in your flesh which otherwise is death.

30 January

When fear comes, pause.

Say what you are afraid of.

Feel the fear.

Breathe.

Take time.

Let love ease you forward from all that holds you rigid.

Let love melt the ice around your heart that holds you from surrender.

Let love loosen you with laughter from the fear of facing your fear.

So you will find that the barriers are lower that are keeping you from trust.

The jump will no longer be fearsomely high.

Have courage.

The Presence is very close and very loving.

31 January

Constant exhortations to be good have little or no effect: they merely add to the burdens of guilt and fear, allies of a cold moralism, rigid and solemn.

Of course you fail.

Relax.

Admit the shams and pretence, the pride and the hiding away, the refusal to let your own truth be seen.

Accept that much failure comes from the difficulty of translating your desire to love into an ability to love well.

So let laughter well up from the deeps, and tears too. Gently shake away the fear, and begin, slowly, to flow again.

1 February

[Andrew Elphinstone struggled some years ago with the impossible questions of evil and pain, writing about them in a book called *Suffering, Freedom, and Love*. He posed this question.]

> Is this a 'Word of God'?
> 'Forgive me for having created a world in which so much pain has to be allowed to happen if I am truly to be a God of Love and enable human beings in freedom to love with a love worthy of the name.'

I'm still moved by that, *and* I want to say, Couldn't you have done better?

2 February

Is forgiveness of one another by human beings too often too cheap?

My heart may become clear of bitterness, so that I no longer let the offence harm me further, and I no longer want revenge.

And I may be open to the possibility of reconciliation with the one who has offended me.

But the *process* of reconciliation cannot happen unless there is genuine repentance, and evidence of the cost of such repentance humbly being paid.

I may refuse to condemn, but it may not be wise
– for both of us – yet to embrace.

3 February

When we receive the forgiveness of another, we are
deeply disturbed.

For the worst in us has been seen and received:
we have not been condemned, exiled, killed, and
yet we know that we have to die – die, that is, to our
own worst selves, not least to the self that is self-
justifying, manipulating, controlling.

The death of condemnation would be easier to
accept.

How dare you accept me as I am? I struggle
with you, refusing that offer, refusing to look you
in the eye which is enduring my offence without
retaliation.

It is so hard to receive forgiveness that is without
conditions – save the costliest: simply to look you in
the eye without blanching.

4 February

To let go of my surface self, my ego self, my control, my power, my self-justifications, yes, it is a dying to self.

Letting go completely is death – and the only way to life.

To receive forgiveness is to prepare ourselves for the final letting go, for the decisive moment of truth, by a little dying, a little letting go.

5 February

To be destitute, deprived, oppressed, enslaved, is to experience a kind of 'damnation' (though it is not a condemnation, for you are not at fault).

You are totally trapped, you have no freedom, you have no power to influence or change events.

To experience 'salvation' is to be enlarged, to enter wide open spaces of freedom, to have the spaciousness and resource to struggle with those who oppress, to fight lovingly with your enemies, in the hope that, one day, they may be embraced as friends.

6 February

Love your enemies: do not condemn them, 'damn' them in your turn, enslave or destroy them.

Keep in contact, even if you cannot keep 'in touch'.

Strive powerfully with them, struggle shoulder to shoulder, and be surprised when you see each other face to face.

Do not yield to bitterness, nor to despair, nor to violence or violation.

Do not categorize or demonize even your worst enemies, classing them as subhuman, thus giving yourself and others permission to maim and to kill.

Beloved enemy…

Be angry if need be, but generously angry, and let your compassion be felt along with your anger, not your hatred.

Dissolve the hatred so easily internalized by believing deep in your own heart that *you are totally loved*.

Protect yourself, yes, do not throw your pearls before swine, be as vulnerable as you dare, but not as a doormat, nor offering your throat to the knife.

Yet look for opportunity to tell your story (for argument never won over an enemy), and the courage you show in being vulnerable will impress and sometimes silence and make thoughtful those who hear.

Love, then, with an expanding heart.

Do not meet oppression with force, for we have all been too much hurt.

Be powerfully and persuasively gentle, with others and with yourself.

Stand (on) your own ground with dignity.

And keep a sense of proportion – and above all a sense of humour.

7 *February*

To all stiff-necked burden-shoulderers:

Let Love guide your embodied being.

(Beware of those who preach grace but impose duty out of guilt.)

Let Spirit flow through you.

Let the government be on God's shoulders.

Hold on to your life – lose it.

Let go of your life – find it.

Let go…

Let be…

Let God…

8 February

Be rooted and grounded in Love, for Love is the Ground of your being.

Be drawn through Love's narrow gate, for Love is the Goal of your becoming.

Take courage, look steadily at yourself, and *love* all of that self.

A character in one of Nikos Kazantzakis' novels uses the image of the larva that dwells deep down in each of us:

> Lean over and say to this larva, I love you,
> and it will sprout wings and become a butterfly.

William Blake wrote:

> We are on this earth
> that we may learn to *bear* the *beams* of love.

Pierre Teilhard de Chardin echoes that:

> Only so can our love for others be a burning gentleness.

Aelred of Rievaulx wrote in the twelfth century:

> If you have no love for your own lasting inter-est, if you hate your own soul (and show it by loving evil), how can you love the very being, the deepest interests, of another?

And Kierkegaard wrote:

> Do not despair, never give up hope for yourself
> or for one another. Bitter enemies and lost
> friends can become friends again. Love that
> has grown cold can kindle and burst into flame.

Be content with the impossibilities, the incompletions, from within which alone the future is shaped and given meaning.

Listen to the whisper of the thunder on a distant shore.

9 *February*

[In his novel *God Knows* Joseph Heller pictures King David ruminating on the answer God gave to Moses when asked his name: 'I am that I am.' Moses is truculent: 'What's that supposed to mean? It doesn't make sense.' And God is heard to reply: 'And where does it say that I'll ever make sense?'

So the invitation is to play with those ancient words, *Ehyeh aser ehyeh*.

With acknowledgment to Martin Buber for some of the ideas in the last part.]

I am that which I am:
I shall be that which I shall be:
That which I am I shall be:
That which I shall be I am.

I shall be there as the One who I there shall be.

I shall be there for you in the unpredictable encounter where for you I shall be there.

You need not cast a spell over me, for I am with you
always, as I always choose to be with you. I do not
assume any of my manifestations beforehand, you
cannot learn to meet me, you meet me when you
meet me.

Then reflect with John the Ruminator on the meaning of *Yeshua*, with the picture language of the ear-
lier part of his work becoming more abstract, less
controllable, the deeper he went.

I AM…
Bread…
Light…
Door…
Shepherd…
Vine…
Way…
Truth…
Life…
Resurrection…

❖

10 February

Here are six body movements – up, down, in, out,
back, forward – along with six praying 'tones': you
may want to add your own.

Reaching up: *'Adoring'*
  Yearning, Leaping.
Reaching down: *'Contemplating'*
  Rooting, Deepening.
Becoming narrow: *'Recognizing'*
  Refining, Dying.
Opening wide: *'Affirming'*
  Expanding, Welcoming, Living, Forgiving.
Reaching backwards: *'Thanking'*
  Remembering, Recalling.
Reaching forwards: *'Trusting'*
  Risking, Venturing.

11 February

My comprehensive task is to be a human being
whose depths are divine.

12 February

'Look for the sunlight in your wood and stone,
look for the skygod in your flesh and bone.'

That close? *That* hidden?

[Apologies. The quotation is ancient, but memory gets worse.
I've forgotten the reference. See 1 September.]

13 February

If biology is *not* destiny, may I be drawn beyond the
past and beyond today, into a greater whole than
any sum of any particular parts.

14 February

Teilhard de Chardin once wrote that humankind
was beginning to look for a way of loving that was
not limited to 'material fecundity'. He called it
'spiritual fecundity'. He hoped that it would more
and more accompany the more familiar procreation
of children, and would ultimately become the only
reason for sexual union.

15 February

Arthur Miller believed that every human being faces a challenge or conflict that, if it were known about, would evoke admiration. Courage is far more widespread than we usually think.

16 February

Mystery is not the unknowable but the inexhaustible.

17 February

The non-violent actions of the peacemakers may protect their self-respect – but nothing more.

18 February

There are two kinds of 'coming out'.

The first is to emerge into the light of day, to come out to play, openly to be a human sexual (of however peculiar a kind), affirming, visible, catholic.

The second is to be separate, to shout into the wind, with nobody listening, nobody hearing the story, nobody in conversation. It is to be fanatical, sectarian, loveless.

19 February

'Become a little child.'

To be like a child in the ancient Mediterranean world of the first century was to be like a woman, like a slave, subject to another's power of life and death, with no power to make any significant decision of your own.

Because of that conventional assumption, that structured fact of life, embedded in law and custom, you cannot be held guilty of the stigma that you live with, you cannot be at fault, you are not to be blamed, you are not to feel ashamed – whatever 'they' say.

When you know what it is like to live under that shadow, you become acutely aware of what comes to you as gift, as grace.

20 February

Dare we pray to be shown how important it is to be useless?

21 February

Do not aim for success or status.

Aim to be where you can live as a sign of salvation for the rejected.

Do not become unavailable to them by becoming acceptable to those who do not like their comfort disturbed.

[From a personal letter from Sister Jane, SLG.]

22 February

If you refuse to use the power you have, you cannot change oppressive ways.

If you use it, you may in turn become oppressor.

Therefore ally your power with the rejected, so that together you may claim your due space.

In so doing, you will have to restrain your own claim to what is more than your due.

But at the same time do not let restraint become so habitual that you give up what is fairly your due.

23 February

You are tempted to look with envy on the younger generation.

But in your turn you have been the privileged inheritor of the strivings of others.

Do not refuse future generations the gift that you alone can give them as you make your unique contribution now.

Whatever the circumstances of time present, each of us enjoys gifts from time past, and each of us is called to sacrifice for the sake of time future.

24 February

I take you into my arms, exhausted, shrivelled baby, gasping for air.

Birthing was nearly too much for you.

I weep for the years I have neglected you, lost child from long ago, yet much loved and much desired.

I take you into my arms and kiss you. I hold you gently, rocking you again, to comfort and to reassure.

You will yet give me life and energy, ever fresh, ever new, colour and warmth where grey decay creeps on insidiously.

I love you, welcome you, nourish you.

25 February

Be alert to the places that once were genuinely life-giving, but are now death-dealing, places that are too constricted now for the growing creature, where the food no longer nourishes, where the energy turns back upon itself, making sour what once gave sweet delight.

There is no other way but forward through another narrow gate, a yearning, shoulder strong but aching, through a dark tunnel into fresh breathing space, a place wide open, free, that once our forebears called 'salvation'.

26 February

So hard not to hurry, driving, walking, washing up, preparing a lesson.

Next time you are *running* late, *walk*.

Next time you are thinking through a problem, wait for the second clarity.

[The last sentence is a thought of Baron von Hügel.]

27 February

Sometimes we act prematurely.

We ask a significant question before the moment is ripe.

We sound off in a tantrum rather than wait until we know how to channel our anger well.

We want excitement now and refuse to give it time to build up to a climax.

We may have been born prematurely or taught in a hothouse.

We come to think that simply because what we do is familiar and frequent it is normal.

Physically, we may be acting too much out of contraction and spasm rather than out of relaxation and rhythm.

Listen for the quieter rhythms; sense the smaller pulsations.

Enjoy them.

They bring their own satisfaction.

Give them time and space.

The major rhythms and the climaxes will then happen in due course, the riding of the great waves, with their own due measure of fulfilment.

❖

28 *February*

When you feel swamped, by attention or power or
love, do not react.

Pause deliberately.

Step back a moment.

Breathe gently.

Stand in your own place.

See the other who loves you or who has power
over you as truly other, and not a reflection of parent or ideology or self.

Then – and only then – *respond*.

29 *February*

Do not deny your own strengths through false
modesty or self-abasement.

Gentleness – meekness even – shows strength
refined and channelled, not denied or concealed.

If you pretend you have no strengths, you will
swing between cruelty and sentimentality, always
the two sides of the one coin.

And others will then be afraid of you and bewil-
dered by you.

1 March

Do not depend on institutions for permission or approval or a ready-made role.

Sense your own ground and dignity and strength, and make your contribution from that ground.

And when you are in role, act in your own way.

Even if you are an ordinary member of an institution, you are part and parcel of it: it is not a 'them'.

You can help to guide its future with passion and compassion.

You have the creative power within you, initiating-nurturing, fathering-mothering.

Take responsibility and shape that power.

There is no need to hold your breath, and draw back in fear.

You have a singular contribution to make.

A loving strength will see you through.

2 *March*

If we human beings are made – or is it 'being made'? – in the divine image – or likeness, and if we can never escape the divine presence, and if we see in Jesus the human face of God – or the embodiment of God – or the Wisdom of God – as flesh and blood, and if this is true for each and all of us, then you are absolutely significant to me, and I am absolutely significant to you, and none of us can be a mere means to an end.

If we do not love our brothers and sisters, our friends and neighbours, our rivals and enemies, we are not loving and cannot love 'God'.

I love you because you are you and because I love God who is in you.

I cannot love you merely as a by-product of my love for God, for I am loving God when I love you.

I am committed to you for ever – even if you slay me…

3 *March*

Do you let yourself 'go through' your experience?

(Or are you 'not all there'?)

We can be content only when full of content – or when we are content to be empty.

4 March

When you seethe inside, terribly accusing of another's faults, feeling superior and remote, listen to
your own angry and needy child within, feel the
self-loathing and the spite, and acknowledge these
things in the presence of someone who loves you.

Then you will be able to respond with humorous
and generous anger, appropriate to whatever injustice is real, to whatever selfishness is actually there.

5 March

Do not suppress your feelings of resentment and
disappointment when someone lets you down.

Do not hide them under a cloak of so-called
unselfishness and concern for the other's welfare.

Such supposed concern is a mask, for you will be
experienced as anxious, aloof, condemning.

The truth is that you are afraid to be angry, and
expect rejection if you are.

6 March

Do not avoid looking in depth at your habitual follies.

It is easier to scrape barnacles off the hull of a boat, expecting it to move more smoothly through the water, than patiently to untangle the weeds choking the anchor chain.

7 March

Let the ice melt from around your heart.

Let the running water melt the icicles of your heart's winter, sharp fear become flowing tears.

Let the presence of another warm you so that the waters of healing may flow.

The ice has formed for your protection, but there comes a time when it is not needed.

And though it will always feel risky to be open and vulnerable again, to say what you feel and what you need, only so can the ice melt, only so can you learn to receive.

Unlike the freezing shock of the first birth, the second birth can be gentle and kindly.

8 March

The eyes, they say, are the windows of the soul.

Sparkling, alive, they want to give and receive.

Anxious, merely existing, they speak volumes of desperate searching, pleading for contact, or they speak of withdrawal inwards, cutting off contact.

And sometimes they flash fiercely, lashing out in cruelty and anger, the life within thwarted and in pain.

9 March

Say Yes to a love that will drag you through the depths, scour your every feeling, scar and heal your heart, lift you to the heights.

10 March

You have loved and lost – in one of the many ways
of 'losing'.

Do not cling.

Now is the time of distancing, of separation –
for the sake of the future, of an impossible union, a
'resurrection from the dead'.

Laughable?

Yet in the Divine Mystery, at an unpredictable
time, at the right time, inevitable.

11 March

You need contact – but not in excess –
or you will be drained.

You need withdrawal – but not in excess –
or you will be frozen.

You need attention – but not in excess –
or you will be smothered.

You need aloneness – but not in excess –
or you will be lonely.

12 March

You loosen your clothing to shit, to pray, to roar, to love, to sleep: the belly needs room to move and relax.

It is hard to be compassionate if you are constipated.

You must let go of your 'up-tight-ness' if you are to give – in or out.

Breathe, don't hold your breath.

Breathe out as far as you can.

Trust that the air will be there to rush in.

Hold on to your life – you will lose it.

Let go of your life – you will find it.

13 March

'I feel safe in your arms.'

'I bet you will do anything I want.'

That is the exchange: complete safety for the one, complete control for the other.

What is missing is risk.

Risk is the companion of faith and adventure – and of growth.

14 March

Ask what you hide and what you show.

Ask what is legitimately private and what is courageously public.

Bring into the public domain what you have learned in private, but find a way of doing so that does not betray the privacy.

When you have lived at the depths, wrestling with meaning, whether the angel you have striven with has been in your dreams or incarnate in your neighbour, find a shape by which to communicate, whether as painting or poem, public servant or presbyter.

The spiritual and the sexual belong together, both privately and publicly.

It is no accident that you grew up in a culture which banned from polite conversation religion, sex, and politics.

15 March

There is always the challenge of the *next* step.

You can refuse it if you wish, and so remain safe.

But you will have retreated within and become chilled one more degree.

Have courage to be vulnerable, not knowing the outcome or the response.

Opportunity and change may provoke fear, and you will risk hurt and failure.

But there is no other way of growing – *growing* old, being creative, making love.

16 March

Bad religion offers safety and security, in the form of a certainty that is the opposite of faith, a control that is the opposite of freedom.

We may *believe* that Divine Love has the resources to meet whatever comes, but we *know* that human love has its limits.

You may not be totally dependable and reliable, I may not be totally safe and secure.

Dare I risk trusting you and loving you, come what may?

Dare you risk loving me?

17 March

Be gentle with your wounds.

Remember that wounds always leave their mark.

The scars may be visible on the skin, or hidden away forgotten.

Some wounds are still harming you, emotional hurts trapped in cell and muscle.

A great shock – or an accumulation of little shocks – can leave you continually wary, watchful, rigid.

On the surface all may seem well: you can slide over the smooth armour that you have put on to protect yourself.

You can get by – not least sexually – with excitement and pleasure.

But the communication you are having with the other remains on the surface.

You cannot know joy.

Be courageous, learn little by little to trust others, that their touching of you more deeply will bring a groan of release, a sigh of peace, a measure of healing.

It may feel like a terrifying risk, you may feel you are about to open yourself to further pain.

But in the end there is no alternative.

18 March

Ask yourself whether or not you are a peacemaker in the politics of the everyday, in family and community, at the heart of conflicts less dramatic than those of the headlines, but on a continuum of human distress and dislocation.

When enough of us work gently, consistently, persistently at the *making* of peace, we may reach 'critical mass'.

We may be helping forward a mutation in the corporate consciousness of humankind.

19 March

Search for meaning, meaning that may come to be adequately (though never perfectly) expressed in words.

Work hard at the task of thoughtful and careful preparation, *towards* discovery.

Only then be expectant that meaning will be *given* to you.

Words lie waiting to be picked up: but you will notice them only if the hard work has been done thoroughly and well.

Then, and only then, can words be fresh-wrought.

Indeed they will then take shape easily as the carrier of truth, will be so accurately angled as to glow with light.

You will look back later and ask, Where did they come from?

20 March

Without words, without listening for the 'wonderful works of God' *in your own language*, your frustration will increase, and you will either hit out in fury or hate yourself into despair.

21 March

Trust in the memory of your best moments.

Keep the memory alive, remind yourself of the stories.

Then, in your worst moments, you will have a resource to draw upon, and there will at least be a chance that your faith-*full*-ness will not be completely drained *empty*.

Trust that everything that is coming to you out of the future will work out for your greater good.

That is faith.

22 March

It is not a bad thing to beat about the bush, having prepared in your heart and mind ideas, images, thoughts, stories.

Of course you *may* be procrastinating.

But it may take time to startle a bird, a phrase, into taking wing.

And though you will not know in advance what kind of bird it will be, even so, follow it.

Catch your story on the wind…

Wait until you are *given* the right word to say.

The words will come if you have the courage to summon them.

[After Laurens van der Post.]

23 March

The Commonwealth of God is constantly present, within you and around you.

The Mysterious Creating One scatters seed, even into the cells of your being: they are the potential for the unexpectedly new.

Seedlings grow towards maturity, whenever you reach out and strive *and* whenever you look within and let be.

Recognize that such a process is also at work in those you draw close to.

Allow that recognition to warm your loving across all the boundaries of age and gender and sexuality, of colour and creed.

Each encounter will enrich your life, making each connection ever more engodded.

24 March

God is greater than you, an ocean to your wave.

You are more than the sum of your parts.

God is more than the sum of all of us.

God is Love inexhaustible.

God is Future, luring, beckoning, towards whom you yearn.

God is within you, Source of your being and of your creativity.

God is between us and among us, invisibly at work, the Presence usually unrecognized.

25 March

Guard and protect your creativity: let the ones you love help you, and in your turn help them.

You need the other and the other needs you to keep alive the divine flame, the Infinite becoming finite through you, coming to birth in you.

There may be many meanings in your loving and your being loved, but this is the most profound and the least selfish: for your love now focuses on the Beyond, on the Future.

Such loving allows time and space for *nothing* to happen.

Resist the temptation to fill the emptiness, even with what is good, for the undoubtedly good may be the enemy of the unpredictably good, and the immediate may squeeze out the vital.

The reward is the deep knowledge that your guardianship has protected the waiting and the silence without which nothing creative happens.

The cost is to persist in the primary loyalty to the Creative Source, each of you recognizing that you need the other to do something that the surface self never likes, which is to be usurped by an unswerving devotion to deeper self, to Deepest Self, to greater good, to Greatest Good.

❖

26 March

For a while, in early days of faith, God may be a Parent to you.

But to this Parent you must not cling.

Before you can discover more, you must separate from the One who gave you new birth.

God withdraws, hides away, and you must let each other be.

Your taking leave of God is as much part of the life of faith as your coming home to God.

And when you give yourself wholly to another, and the other to you, you will discover the God who is already there before you.

27 March

Let your love for each other be exclusive, not in the sense of 'excluding', but of 'special'.

It is not that you matter to each other more than any*thing* else in the world, nor that you matter to each other more than any*one* else in the world, (though that may be so), but that you matter to each other in a unique way that nobody can replace, and *that* matters to both of you very much indeed.

The other who *matters* may not be indispensable, but is always irreplaceable.

28 March

You *say* that you want to claim him exclusively *for you* – such is the total demand of inloveness.

But he cannot fill the aching void that has opened up inside you, which you did not know existed until you fell in love and knew the emptiness you feel when you are apart.

Because the void cannot be filled by him you face the challenge of living *within* and *from* that void, bearing the ache in ever-deepening love *for* him and *for* everybody else in your life.

And because no human being can fill that void, cheap religion claims that God can fill it, as if the Divine were an instant painkiller.

Rather is it that by living from the centre and depth of that void the Divine Life and Love grow *in* you and come to be expressed *through* you.

Inloveness is heady and delightful, but sours if and when you try and hold to 'it' or 'him'.

Then it becomes possessiveness.

You have no control over when you fall in love, but it always brings with it temptation, test, and trap.

It brings with it an avoidance of truth, a setting up of the other as an idol, an escape from the true intimacy which tolerates and needs space between, a false simplification of life, blissfully but temporarily seeming to solve all your problems.

Inloveness makes irrational demands and blind excuses: it refuses the *truth-in-love*.

Such love is honest about what is *inevitable* – fear and anger, disappointments and griefs, let-downs if not betrayals.

Love – but only at its deepest and best, prolonged, sustained – can contain and transform all the unexpected energies unleashed by falling in love.

29 March

Let there be space between you.

Remember that the ones you love in your heart are but guests in your soul.

Do not claim too much from him, anything that is beyond the integrity of his giving.

He may indeed be steadfast and loyal to you, but he cannot give (and you cannot therefore receive) if you do not withdraw your projections.

He may bear with your weaknesses, but you must bear with the anxieties that rise up within you and have nothing to do with him.

Much 'noise' from your past gets in the way of truthful loving.

He may give you protection and encouragement as you dare to listen closely to that noise, but he cannot do the work that you alone must do before you can hear music rather than clamour, and learn to distinguish true-love from in-love.

30 March

It may not feel like a precious gift, but his love for you while not in love with you, is a gateway to greater maturity.

Ask him to keep in touch, frequently but in small ways – a postcard will do every week or two – because you cannot bear too much separation yet.

Be clear about it, and do not ask for anything else.

This will free his giving, which can be honest and relaxed.

Otherwise he will be disturbed by you and afraid of the power of your desire to possess.

Negotiate the boundaries and the limits, and within the container your ability to trust will grow, along with the conviction that *you* are loved.

Feel the fear you have of rejection, the fear, too, of unconditional love, of being understood and forgiven.

Feel your grief and anger, letting them be warm, not cold.

Do not let them shrivel you into bitterness.

Be willing to bear together the agony and the glory of being human.

❖

31 March

There is a mature innocence on the yonder side of experience and suffering.

It is the innocent love that no longer desires to harm, a love that is always more trustworthy than passionate love.

Projections, idols, mirrors are no longer mixed up with it.

1 April

Do not seal off your heart for fear of the hollow at the centre, of the griefs of years past, of the anger of your passion.

Open-heartedness hurts – sometimes it is the pain of surgery.

Keep loving through the hurt, opening your heart to a transformation from cold-hearted to warm-hearted.

2 April

The many cannot avoid the paid work that keeps the world moving, the kinds of work that are similar everywhere, not least the cleaning of streets, offices, parks, homes, and the maintenance of buildings and the administration of institutions, in the service of health and education and local authorities.

Only a few can find paid work (and sometimes the pay is little if at all) which is unique to them, in which their singularity can flourish.

They are the artists and clowns, the future-bearers.

The rest of the community depends on them to take life forward, so that it does not become stuck in endlessly repeated routines.

They of course depend on the others for their food, shelter, clothing, and care.

It may be that the work of the many is a job and the work of the few a vocation.

It may be that we are all 'called' to both chores and creativity.

And if 'God' is everywhere or nowhere, then a job has as much value as a vocation.

❖

3 April

Let your tendrils reach into a future that is nothing
and dark and totally unknown.

4 April

Be a nonsense, a symbol of that which does not fit.
(Does evolution actually depend on the survival of
that which at present is not the 'fittest', that doesn't
fit in?)

5 April

Abhorrence and fear make it impossible for us to
listen to those who provoke those feelings.
    This is the emotional dynamic of so many
clashes on issues of sexuality.

6 April

The pebble in your hand puts a millennium in
perspective.

7 *April*

A place, a project, a job, an experiment, a chapter of a life – each has its dawning, noon, and afternoon.

If you do not move on when the time is ripe, the advancing shadows will spread their murk.

And, to spin a fancy, murk turns to muck when you put the leftovers on the compost heap, all that has not been digested.

Do not take too much of the past with you

Let it lose its identity, mixed in with the soil, lost so that something new may be fertilized.

8 *April*

The jewel of wealth and display may signify a great love, but makes its owner vulnerable to attack and adds to the income of insurers.

The jewel of a shaft of sunlight piercing the mist cannot be grasped or thieved or bought or taken away.

Like the passing scent of summer, like human praise, it is to be enjoyed, but not inhaled.

[Acknowledgment to Basil Hume for that last thought.]

9 April

Plato thought that we may well choose the circumstances of our lives.

'AE' (George Russell) wrote of 'the secrecy of our being', where, hidden from our outer selves, we *will* the understanding that may come from what that outer self thoroughly dislikes – suffering, imprisonment, rejection.

It is difficult to distinguish this from the hidden places whence come our repeated, compulsive, destructive actions.

These, however, can be recognized by a use of power that dominates rather than power that enables freedom; a wasting of time; the deceptions and lies that always obstruct wisdom; a dynamic of irrational guilt and self-hatred; a reinforcement of isolation and detachment, the opposite of relationship, community and communion; a simultaneous assertion of surface self and flight from true self.

10 April

Whenever you catch yourself saying to someone, 'You deserve it', you may be exaggerating an achievement on the principle of I scratch your back, you may scratch mine, or you may be trying to justify a secret indulgence of your own, or you may, with the opposite meaning, be justifying a punishment.

Usually it is yourself that is at the centre, and your heart is either collusive or cold, distorted or embittered.

11 April

When you experience tension, you are engaging in solo tug-of-war, even if the perceived goal in each direction is a good one.

Either one wins and the other loses, or you collapse exhausted, yourself and the rope in a heap.

Stand your ground.

Drop your centre of gravity.

Sense a deeper strength.

Instead of being pulled in two directions, look for a third, more unifying, goal.

It may be that neither currently perceived goal is what you most deeply desire.

You will then have the energy to contain the tension.

When you become aware at that deep level, you will find that you can throw the rope away.

12 April

Violation includes violence, all the obvious forms of brutality, cruelty, destruction, force.

But there are less obvious forms.

There is manipulation, often subtle, usually hidden.

There is stigmatizing, which is a structured bias, putting people into a labelled category that is automatically deemed inferior, ignoring character and talent.

There is the deliberate withholding of warmth and affection.

There is the 'stunning' brilliance of good looks and wealth.

There is the 'spell-binding' eloquence of oratory.

Each humiliates, dehumanizes, annihilates.

13 April

Ask yourself:

Would I be at ease eating a meal with…?

(Complete with a name or a face.)

If not, why are you uneasy?

Is it that you wouldn't know what to say?

Is it that your reputation might suffer?

In which direction would you wish to move?

Towards apart-heid?

Toward con-viviality?

14 April

In Dante's *Inferno* the courtesans are with the forgers.

Both deal in counterfeit.

They disrupt, they confuse, they block the flow of true love and genuine coinage.

15 April

Have you ever prayed as a Jewish mystic challenged?

Before you pray, make sure your will is in order.

16 April

To go through a narrow gate is to have accepted constriction, restraint, limitation, a refusal of other possible gates.

There is only one way left.

Now is the time to take your unique path, and it always includes a dying.

Nothing will ever be the same again.

There is no way back.

17 April

Put the work first, the task that is greater than you, that will always defeat you.

Put all your energy into it, everything that you have.

Spend that energy until there are no coins left.

Then it will be the right time to die, not at a moment of clock time dictated by disease and decay, but at a moment of significant time, when dying is simply the next thing you have to do.

(Few manage it this way, for we find it so hard to will one thing and only one.)

18 April

If I reject you, I lose part of myself.

If you reject me, you lose part of yourself.

If we disagree, we are not rejecting each other, as long as neither of us pushes away or draws back, as long as we are glad to be seen together, and as long as we are not using our power in an 'over-against' way.

Therefore, I have to lay aside my power if I am to receive and not to reject you.

Only so will I discover that lost part of myself.

And the same is true for you in relation to me.

19 April

You are engaged on a task.

You have not allowed enough time for it.

You begin to hurry.

You now care more about something that may happen in the future than you do about the task.

You have begun to be elsewhere rather than here, then rather than now.

20 April

When you pass a good-looking person in the street, and you mutter (or think) 'Wow!' or 'Grr!' it is hard to let go and recognize the very next person as equally loved by God (and therefore by you?).

Such is our habitual order of priorities: Our desires; other people insofar as they can satisfy our desires; other people in themselves, but only insofar as they are a pleasure to be with; other people in themselves, period; others, with ourselves, equally significant in God.

To become holy is to work through your desires and reach the point where you no longer calculate.

21 April

To succumb to 'accidie' is to become lazy, sullen, morbid, hard-hearted, self-centred.

Its opposite is 'com*punc*tion', a kind of '*punc*turing', a piercing of the huge balloon of false self, a piercing of the heart, a cutting to the quick.

What helps?

Do some simple physical work.

Phone a neighbour.

Remember you may die tonight.

Intend to change even when you don't *feel* the desire.

Keep on praying – gently.

22 April

O Thou No-Thing because of Whom there is Every-thing.

O Thou No-One because of Whom there is Every-one.

O Thou Empty Space in which we learn to dance.

O Thou Bottomless Pit down which we learn to soar.

23 April

If you know a deep inner peace, people will find their way to you.

The desperate will want to snatch at that peace, however unaware they may be that they are intent on devouring you.

They will need to stay within range, but find and inhabit their own space, at present full of fury or empty of meaning.

In contrast, the shy will want to keep their distance, hesitant, afraid of being touched.

They will need to come closer, to trust that you will not take over their space, to allow themselves room to breathe deeply near you.

Both actions need courage.

Discerning which is appropriate at what time is not easy.

24 April

Still the whirring wings of your thoughts, the ceaseless buzzing round your brain.

Fold the wings across your chest, that your heart may be warmed and hatched.

25 *April*

The contemplative monks and nuns were recommended to pray their way into the constrictions of their small cells until they knew the cell as a place of freedom.

It may be there is a wisdom in choosing to close a door before a door is closed upon you – by ill health, redundancy, the loss of a limb.

The challenge is to *realize* freedom from *within* your cell.

And a death bed is the final cell.

26 *April*

Rilke took the image of the cell excruciatingly further.

For him, the artist is a dancer whose movements are broken against the walls of the cell.

Do we have to trim our movements to the boundaries that press upon us?

Do foot steps and arm sweeps have to be scaled down to exquisite miniature?

Is there some truth discoverable only when words are fresh wrought on parched exhausted lips?

Rilke bids the dancer: Stretch the unlived lines of your body into the walls with your wounded fingers.

27 *April*

If you are isolated and cannot believe in Love – because of your own or other people's persistent folly or malice or neglect, you will be afraid that by letting go of hard-won control you will fall into a Bottomless Pit of Terror rather than into an Unfathomable Abyss of Love.

28 *April*

Let your touch be gentle, warm, content not to seize or grab, tightly holding.

Let your touch be leisurely and lingering, accurate in its discerning.

Let your touch be honest and genuine, flowing outwards from the centre of truth within.

Let your touch come from the diffusion of loving energy throughout the flesh-body.

Such touch is a divinely given and divinely charged means of reaching out and drawing close.

29 April

Which part of the flesh-body can you trust me
with?

Which part of the flesh-body can I trust you
with?

❖

30 April

What do you make known?

What do you keep secret?

What do you keep, if not secret, at least private?

Can 'the secrets of all hearts be disclosed' without 'casting pearls before swine'?

How do you find the path between 'bottling it all
up' and 'spilling the beans'?

If you tell your story, you are at other people's
mercy.

If you do not tell your story, your life washes
away.

Meaning comes from stories told and received.

Without exchange we waste away and fade,
shades of our ancestral selves.

❖

1 May

You are unique.

You are alone.

You soliloquize.

You write.

You retire into your inner cell.

But there is a world of difference between a recluse, hating humankind, trying to have nothing to do with others, and a hermit, loving humankind, in solidarity with others.

Externally, they may look the same, for each lives alone.

Internally, the difference is precisely that the hermit cherishes *everything* and e*verybody* in the heart, and, when opportunity offers, engages in dialogue with others, without which human beings do not grow.

Hermits-in-pairs, venturing forth from time to time, nourish the common life.

2 May

The more you are truly yourself, the less power you will have over others; and even that which you have will be taken away.

3 May

The more you refuse the burden of your own struggle, the weightier will be the burden that others have to bear.

And if you bear the burden *in* 'God', the yoke will be easy, the burden light.

4 May

Your gifts to me may be hidden.

I may find you a nuisance, a bother, mildly (or not so mildly) irritating.

It may be hard to go beneath my sense of you as a burden.

I need to keep focused on my will to love, and the sheer fact that you are a human being, and that you are here, now, with me.

Will such an exercise of love train me into loving those who have harmed me, whom I distrust?

Central to my awareness needs to be the Divine Love that embraces us both.

5 May

Whenever and wherever you relate to others, from one to millions, you will oppress others when your power and authority *systematically* imposes burdens and penalties on those who are less powerful than you are.

6 May

The world of assumptions into which we were born distinguishes between 'one of us' and 'not quite one of us', not our type…class…religion…race…sexuality, who are not quite fully human, who do not deserve our respect.

It is but an easy step to actions based on that assumption – or, more subtly, not to protest, colluding in silence when others so act.

The logic leads to the concentration camp, and to ethnic slaughter.

Never call it 'ethnic *cleansing*', however subtly tempting it is to 'wipe the slate clean', not to have to relate to the different and the strange.

We are all 'impure', mixed together, often enough 'mixed up', in fact, mongrels.

7 May

The opposite of the harmonious and well-ordered is the chaotic and dis-ordered, not the wild and untamed.

They have their own reasons – as does the human heart.

8 May

Rituals sometimes serve to confirm an order of things which is comfortable: they send us out to the rest of our lives strengthened but complacent.

Rituals sometimes serve to overturn an existing order: they disturb the comfortable and send us out determined to shake up the complacent.

Do you seek 'con-firm-ation', at its best 'making us strong together'?

Or do you also want the familiar to prepare you for the gift (not always immediately desired) of the unfamiliar, the moments of 'trans-form-ation' cutting across the accepted forms?

9 May

There are now no places on earth *untouched* by human *impact*, not even the remotest of wilder-nesses.

The human presence may be invisible or second-hand, via radiation on the wind or electronic pulses from satellites.

Nevertheless, it is a *real presence*.

But for good or ill?

10 May

You are Grounded in Being.

You are a Wave in the Ocean.

And you are also addressed, called, lured, drawn asby a magnet, invited, courteously and irresistibly, Come, and become.

It is given by the One who is Other, something like a True Lover, simply, Thou.

I-and-Thou – and also All-Is-One.

Paradox.

11 May

You may believe firmly in life after death, in the continuing identity of your *true* self, recognizable and recognizing, spiritually embodied, beyond the confines of space and time.

However, for all practical purposes, here and now you have no need of that belief.

Lay it on one side, put it in the attic – lest you cease to care for the earth, lest you do not learn how to die, lest you use religion as drug or prop, lest you refuse to enter places of emptiness and desolation, where there is no nourishment or consolation, where *all* seems destined for *nothing*.

Then, yonder, *nothing* may be *all*.

12 May

Hell is the awareness of being separated from Love but is never beyond the reach of Love.

13 May

You can walk away from an awkward question or you can walk along with an awkward question.

Do not hurry into a premature answer.

Rather, slowly and deliberately hold and bear with the question, persistently but gently delving it.

That is what it means to walk in a sacred manner.

14 May

If one layer of unhappiness, restlessness, anxiety is removed, the next inevitably comes to the surface.

Even if there may be interludes between bouts of engaging with personal distress, the constant murmur of the world's pain impinges upon us.

Since we cannot separate ourselves from others, how might we bring the note of unhappiness to those of other voices, other musical notes, those that give us moments of bliss and joy, and, as in a duet, let the notes of unease contribute to a melody more profound than anything the world has yet heard?

15 May

It is not that your relationship with God is primary while that with other human beings is always secondary.

Rather is it that you encounter God *in* and *through* such human relationships.

But if those relationships are false and debased, you will not be encountering *God*, who is present in the deeper, often hidden, places, where love and truth are met.

It is love and truth which signal the divine presence, inextricably mixed in with the human and rarely distinguishable from it.

16 May

It is one of life's sorrows that only rarely, and even more rarely, for long, that we find ourselves able to rest secure in the heart of another.

17 May

Love, sleep, and truth resent too direct an approach.

Do not be hasty in revealing the 'naked' truth.

Do not be indiscriminate in telling your story, neither what you say nor to whom you say it.

Tell your story carefully, indirectly, tactfully.

Discern the difference between the tenderly erotic and the hard pornographic.

18 May

Throw yourself away – you will disintegrate.

Give yourself away – you will become integrated.

19 May

Love the distance between you, whether caused by temperament, or by geography, or by death.

20 May

Try to force your way and nothing real will come
your way.

    Wait.

    Look.

    Listen.

    (That's an item from the Spiritual Highway
Code.)

    What you need will be given – provided you
genuinely desire your deepest need.

    The gift will undoubtedly be a surprise.

21 May

Let the seed germinate.

    Give it its own time.

    You can't see it.

    It has as yet no other form than seed.

    To dig it up as it germinates is to kill it.

    It needs time to root.

    Even when a seedling appears, you will not know
how it will flower, let alone how it will fruit.

    The most you can do is gentle watering.

    The best you can be is patient.

22 May

When you are offering your *singular* contribution to the common good, you will have already come to terms with a measure of *solitariness*.

Many will resist your gift, because they are still trapped by their fear of being *alone*, as well as their fear of 'standing' 'out' from the crowd.

It may be that only the next generation will be able to receive what you are giving.

That will bring you a new kind of *loneliness*, a cost which you have to bear, and a discomfort into which you will have to lower yourself gently – and so discover a greater ease, a more spacious freedom, in ever deepening *solitude*.

23 May

Is our deepest yearning for a 'God' who has not yet appeared?

Or for a revelation of 'God' who is as yet unknown, who is simply 'Future'?

A form of belief that seems complete, 'all of a piece', whether defined by a canon of sacred texts, or by a creed, or by interlocking bricks of doctrine, claims that everything important has already been given.

Its danger is that it claims finality when it is at best provisional.

The *life* in it – that which is important, indeed essential, seeps away, and you are left with a dry husk.

The Spirit of the Ages has moved on, seeking to be shaped anew *in* and *through* us, here and now.

The new may be consonant with, connected with, the best of the old, but it cannot be identical to it.

Otherwise all creativity, human and divine, has ceased.

24 May

You are overwhelmed by sorrow, perplexed, speech-less.

You draw back, retire into yourself, draw down the blinds.

At best you plod, softening the pain by simple routines, your steps echoing the dull thud within.

Rilke would have us believe that it is precisely at such a time that something new, unknown, as yet unrecognized, enters our being, to begin a work of transformation, something that will prove crucial to our destiny.

25 May

That which is most difficult in your life, that produces in you struggle and anxiety, that seems to be most hostile to your well-being, that may be terrifying and giving you sleepless nights, once recognized, may be something helpless that needs your arms of compassion, may be the bearer to you of needful gifts, may come to be your closest ally and friend in whom you put your greatest trust.

26 May

There is no need to make an exhausting effort to try and prove you are of worth.

In any case the attempt is impossible.

All you do is, like Sisyphus, repeatedly push a boulder up a hill, only to find it keeps on rolling down again.

You *are* dearly loved.

You *are* of infinite worth.

You *are* marvellous and wonderful.

It is only when your forget those truths that things go wrong.

The Divine Voice says, I take great delight in you.

All you have to do is to wake up and open your eyes.

27 May

Wait like the birdwatcher, silent, attentive, for who-ever and whatever is approaching to reveal itself.

Aletheia, the Greek for 'truth', means 'an un-covering'.

Give attention, then, to that which *is other than you*, while never being entirely *separate from you*.

By this simple attention, this contemplation, which is the very opposite of grabbing at the other, shaping it to fit your own little mould, you will be transfigured.

Great art, holy people, divine mystery – they do this in you if you *give yourself* enough into the attention.

[After Alan Jones.]

28 May

You claim you are righteous.

You show by that claim that you are cruel.

You claim to love others for their good.

You show by that claim that you manipulate.

You claim to be just.

You show by that claim that you are not free from being vengeful and vindictive.

Dare you claim to be free of all desire to shame, to torture, to humiliate, to see others writhe and squirm, to treat them as refuse?

It is yourself that you really hate.

Denying that you have ever felt and acted in these dehumanizing ways, you are denying part of the truth about yourself.

And whether you admit it or not, you are a node in an interconnecting web of power, you make an explicit or implicit contribution to economic, political, and social structures that treat some human beings as at best inferior, and at worst less than human, and consequently expendable, disposable.

29 May

Be quietly attentive to what is happening within you and within the other, and allow the truth to show itself between you.

Be midwives to each other's struggle and hope in the birthing of new life.

30 May

Become aware of the Devourer, the insistent drives on the loose, the unconscious compulsions that surface as habits, then addictions, the gobbling of people and ideas, the restless desire to dominate, to control, to comprehend.

It is a terrible and destructive use of *power*.

31 May

Detach yourself from everything you project on to others, so that you may see them as they truly are.

May your vision be luminously clear, without fantasy or delusion.

1 June

Recognize that the inevitabilities of your behaviour – the besetting, repeated, often petty wrongdoings, which you waste time in committing and then waste more time in breast-beating about them – can best be understood as signals of a love and presence that will humble you by accepting you, but will not humiliate you by dominating you, however much you feel dominated by your lesser desires.

Such a recognition is the gateway to that inner peace which draws together for good all that you really desire and which your wrongdoings obscure and hinder.

2 June

To pray, to participate in the process of 'patient attention' and 'passionate engagement', is to be willing to place yourself on the threshold of death, and to wait there, so that new life may come to birth in you and through you.

The new born child will hold your hand and will both warm and encourage you.

That child is close relative to your own neglected inner child who does not quite believe that your 'children' are welcome and their gifts appreciated.

[The first two phrases are from Alan Ecclestone in his classic *Yes to God*.]

3 June

The mist clears to give you hope.
The mist descends to test your faith.

4 June

Jesus saw and lived out a vision.

Some of those who met him glimpsed that vision too and, fitfully, lived it.

But from the outset, they began to organize the vision, and so betrayed it.

That is always so.

Now, as then, the vision is our glory; the betrayal is our tragedy.

5 June

Tears soften the limescale of your being, refresh your shrivelled heart, still your agitated mind, clear the eye of your perception.

Thus softened and stilled, refreshed and cleansed, you can will the one thing needful.

6 June

If you know more than you can embody, you have to unlearn by suffering.

7 June

If you demand too much of yourself, your self will demand you recognize how partial you are (in both senses, limited as well as biased).

8 June

'Soul' is not a thing, a substance, an entity, not even your indestructible core, (like the bone we call the 'sacrum', which was once believed to be indestructible, from which would grow the 'resurrection body').

'Soul' is your self, under the movement of pressure, not least the pressures of your pains and contradictions, which at best evoke the trust that there is a greater power than you that will keep you moving in the right direction.

'Soul' is an energy difficult for 'body' to contain.

'Body' often disperses that energy, which cannot therefore do its work towards transforming 'body'.

The real you can so easily miscarry.

9 June

Be content with a divided mind, for the precise mind, without doubt or indecision, persecutes.

Be content with an uneasy conscience, for the supposedly guiltless conscience scapegoats and commits atrocities with an easy mind.

Be content with a sense of failure, for success puts you above others, and seduces you into ideologies.

[After Graham Greene.]

10 June

So many questions have no answers.

So much suffering cries out with no response.

There is so much injustice in the world.

Let us be angry, but with one another, not at one another.

[After Elie Wiesel.]

11 June

Wake up from the delusion of the ego, not least from 'inlovenesses' – from Adonises to alcohol – for even what is natural and can be good deludes when it becomes the only good in your life.

At first the waking up is to darkness, not light, aloneness, not companionship.

What is happening is that you are falling into an abyss of faith which cannot yet be felt as love.

Be glad that you can never reach the bottom of that abyss – for that would be to break upon the false rocks of certainty.

As Iris Murdoch once said, take that 'never' 'for your hope and your shield and your most glorious promise'.

12 June

Stuart Jackman at the end of his novel *The Davidson Affair* wrote that we prefer to be in prison and do not want to be rescued.

W. H. Auden wrote that we prefer to be ruined than to change, we prefer to 'die in our dread' than 'see our illusions die'.

13 June

Allow the pain, the frustration, the unresolved questions, the unsatisfied desire.

If there is no action you can genuinely take, allow these realities to *be*.

Do not fight against them.

Accept that for now there is no calm, clarity, or control.

Keep wondering (in one sense if not yet in the other) through the pain, continuing to ponder, and determined not to deny the possibility of marvel.

Ponder the Mystery at the Heart of all Life, the Wounded but Persistent Heartbeat, the Pinioned Wings.

Desire the impossible at this moment, the desire to grow in love, but do not *try* to do anything about it.

Let your whole being stretch into its cry of passion, ringing and being wrung through you.

14 June

Everyday life and work includes chores and routines.

It also includes that which comes from dedication to whoever or whatever is other than you and greater than you.

It includes inner exploration, the personal journey towards meaning, to *some* extent seeking to understand, to a greater extent *heart*-work.

It includes making connections – the networks of affection, concern, and, as prayer, intercession, weaving and mending the threads that hold us together in the Divine Love.

And it is to do all these things personally and informally, corporately and organizationally, and to focus them in rites of passage and other rituals.

15 June

Why can't I ever completely know you?

How can I learn to love the space between us, the yawning gaps, the unfathomable chasms?

How can I keep in touch when we have wounded each other?

Friendship, whether with God or human being, cannot be true and lasting until is has lived through those questions.

16 June

Mysterious One, you are open to me; you let your-self be affected by me; you suffer with me, from me, for me, in passionate love for me; you let yourself be humiliated because you are tenacious in your love for me.

In the rift of your heart my heartbreak finds a home.

In the rift of my heart you choose to set up the tent of your dwelling.

17 June

Each figure is complete.

Each inclines towards the other.

The three incline towards the one who is drawn to the empty place at the table.

Each is free.

Each is loving.

They belong together in a unity greater than each, and greater than the sum of them.

[On the Rubliev icon of the Three Angelic Messengers.]

18 June

May a loving heart grow in you, burning with love
for the whole of creation, for men and women and
children, for the birds, for the beasts, for the demons.

Radiate a fleshly warmth.

Suffer in solidarity, with an immense compassion.

Come down to earth in material and bodily care.

[Mostly St Isaac the Syrian.]

19 June

The old cloth is unravelling, and we do not yet
perceive the new pattern.

Some of the threads will disintegrate into dust,
their life and purpose being over.

Other threads may be renewed by dipping them
into dye.

And in our generation we are called to be spin-
ners of new threads.

A few will try out tentative, provisional designs,
at first on paper.

The next generation, being born now at a turn
in time, will be the weavers.

[I owe the metaphor in the first sentence to Gilbert Shaw and
Mary Clare SLG.]

20 June

Nephesh is Hebrew for 'en-spirited', 'im-passioned'.

It is never *passion* that is the source of evil, but greed, hard-heartededness, callousness.

21 June

Let the pieces of the faded mosaic be pulled away gently from the wall.

Do not throw them away.

You will need some of them for new patterns, even if you cannot yet discern the design.

You may feel you are disintegrating into fragments.

But even fragments can be gathered, whether of stone or bread.

Maybe a larger self, a soul-body, needs them all.

22 June

To be virgin is to be continuously open, to keep available a space within into which you can invite another, perhaps to bear that person's temporary helplessness, that he or she may be born (again and again) – or be borne – in and into God.

It is to be a God-bearer.

It is to accept that the intimate presence of an-other will cause you pain.

It is to be glad that others can find in your open space the room they need in order, at last, to breathe freely.

23 June

In the 'Krisis' through which the world is passing, when many *fall* by the wayside, perhaps the only choice we have is in *how* we fall, resistant, rebellious, afraid, or welcoming, obedient, trusting.

24 June

The *grip* of evil: the inordinate rather than the bal-anced; the delusory rather than the truthful; the solemn rather than the light-hearted; the frozen rather than the warm-hearted; being held by the reflection in a mirror of distortion.

The names are legion: revenge, hatred, malice, greed; the cold look in the eyes; small pulses of desire that you hardly notice, yet which trigger far-reaching deeds.

And we can think of the *net* of evil, in which we are together enmeshed, more powerful than the sum of individual actions, more powerful it seems than the human race's wisdom to deal with.

Such a net is loosened by humility, truth, laughter, compassion, a usually invisible Spirit working to the pattern of the Christ.

25 June

Original sin is a pervasive **d**is-orientation whereby life is *organized* for **d**ecay, **d**isaster, **d**estruction, **d**eadliness.

When those '**d**'s bring about shattering events, we are fascinated, held in *thrall* by the screen.

We, subtly and hidden, or brazenly and openly, **d**eeply **d**esire, for others and for ourselves, such **d**isintegration and **d**oom.

[After William McNamara.]

26 June

You allure me, you draw me by an invisible but powerful thread, into the wilderness, into the desert, so that there you may speak to my heart.

[After Hosea 2.14.]

27 June

You carry *within* you the tumultuous and tender God, the awesome and intimate God, the implacable and gentle God.

28 June

Be recollected, gathered together, totally present, mind-full, care-full, in each particular of everyday life.

The opposite of that is to be irreligious, not religious (as if in a special compartment separate from the everyday).

Do you want your religious way to be an escape from ordinary life or a way of living ordinary life in all its abundance and full-ness?

29 June

To *grasp* is to know, to control.
To *touch* is to receive and respond.
Which *way* leads to understanding,
to under-standing, to wisdom?

30 June

On pilgrimage, which is more important, the destination or the journey?

Do you want to accomplish, to arrive, or to become more aware as you travel, to be surprised?

Will you hurry by the clock, or dawdle at leisure?

Is the meaning given by the history of the place you travel to, or is it discovered in the presences of the journey?

Is it more like 'work' or like 'play?

David Steindl-Rast calls contemplative life 'ascetical leisure'.

So oases and inns are necessary for pilgrims, as are delays and the weather that keeps you indoors.

1 July

David Steindl-Rast points out that we can choose 'absurdity' (which is derived from *ab-surdus*, 'completely deaf') or 'obedience' (which is derived from *ab-audiens*, 'listening with the heart attuned to the deepest meaning').

The more you are willing to listen, the more you will be drawn into silence.

2 July

In contemplation, you are 'given over' to loving and patient attention to what is, waiting for a gift of meaning.

From contemplation, you 'give yourself over' to passionate engagement with what is given, so to shape it as a gift to others.

You 'empty yourself' in the process.

You have continually to trust that, as when you breathe out, the air will be already there to fill your lungs again.

3 July

The deeper you dig, the wider will be your influence.

Be deeply committed, and widely open.

4 July

As a 'hermit', as a 'prophet', as a 'monk' pioneering the Way, as a 'fool' dancing on the edge, you need a 'bishop' to keep an eye on the whole, (to 'over-see'), to hold you and others together, to be 'sym-bolic', bringing together opposites, not 'dia-bolic', fragmenting and splitting apart.

You also need a 'bishop' to guard your boundaries, to keep the bullies and persecutors at bay, and to help and encourage in hard times.

Such a person in such a role in such a relationship with you will enhance and not restrict your freedom.

Authority at its best is not that which frustrates and against which you chafe, but a wise provision for recognizing human limitations, and enabling human flourishing.

5 July

If you are self-conscious about prayer, you are likely to become pious and priggish.

If you are God-conscious about life, you are likely to to become devoted and delightful.

You will seem atheist, but will be close enough *to* God to keep quiet *about* God (most of the time).

6 July

The survival of the fittest is not necessarily the survival of the physically strongest, of the most powerful, of the gymnastically fit.

It is the survival of that which is most fitted and fitting, in the circumstances, to survive.

And that may be to be weak in the eyes of the strong, vulnerable in the sights of the armoured, open in the squint of the protected.

For those who are most powerful, defended, and shielded are the most isolated.

They are the least available to love, and because they do not travel light, and are above themselves, when they fall, they have the furthest to tumble, and do so most heavily.

On a fragile planet they are least fit for survival.

7 July

May Sarton wrote of what those who live alone know well.

When guests depart, there is a time of loneliness before 'the solitude opens' again.

8 July

You feel incomplete, unfruitful.

Do not fret about it.

Accept it.

Be at peace with it.

Allow a greater completion and fruitfulness to grow in you unknown and unseen.

The only way you can stop that greater process is by trying to understand it.

[After Thomas Merton.]

❖

9 July

The mountain, implacable, says, Choose.

To choose is to say a wholehearted No (even to what is good) for the sake of a more wholehearted Yes (to a greater good) without knowing in advance what that Yes will entail.

Having said Yes you sense your strength, and you can lie back and enjoy the mountain's solid embrace.

❖

10 July

At the everyday level, you may be *merely* alone or *merely* next to another.

At the creative level, you are *with* yourself, and you are *with* others.

You are grounded in the depth of being, in silence, in solitude, and when you are with others, you recognize the Presence of the Go-Between.

11 July

Detach yourself from the busy-ness of too many distractions and too many commitments, however good and justifiable they are.

You will no longer be dispersing energy.

You can begin to go deep enough to be graced by Presence.

12 July

Drop your weight into the Ground of your being, into the Mysterious Presence, and only then let the firm, gentle, and loving energy rise up and flow into whatever it is you are required to do.

13 July

Set your feet in a large room, in the expanse of landscape.

Walk gently and slowly, more and more aware of Silence, Mystery, Being, Presence.

Realize the slowing down of time, the clarity of the ordinary, the slow turnings of the road.

You are walking to no purpose, no decided and necessary destination.

Saunter to your *Sainte Terre*, not to the 'holy lands', there and then, but to the realities, the sacredness, of here and now.

14 July

Enjoy the American Indian child in you, who exults in wild and empty places, where the adult you is top heavy and ill at ease, the child who is lithe and graceful and at home in the land, by name, Laughing Water.

15 July

C. S. Lewis described the new Narnia as a '*deeper* country' than the old, where every feature 'meant more'.

Charles Wesley wrote of '*solid* joys'.

The truly spiritual is not more airy, but more rooted.

Our destiny is not to be wispy ghosts, but transformed *bodies*.

16 July

We are dismayed only when we feel isolated – by pain, by a secret burden, by shame, by stigma, by being on our own – when we lose all sense of connection (and direction).

The *reality* is that we connect with everybody and everything, always and everywhere.

We are bound to be unaware of most of those connections most of the time, physically separated as we are by oceans and by death.

But we do well to remember that such awareness will come and go, and not to be downcast when we cannot see or hear the others.

Be expectant that the awareness will return, and that today you will be surprised.

17 July

Are you really free when you are doing what you want, or when you really want to do what you most truly believe you must?

18 July

You may be particularly aware that the place where you tread is sacred ground.

Let that awareness spread so that you see the sacred at least potential in every ground.

Take greatest care when your sense is not of Presence but of Absence.

This is the place ready to be made sacred now.

19 July

How do you speak and write?

At what level?

From what depth?

Dreaming of fame and wealth?

Or a way that will not harm you?

Your ego self will stain your work, will feed your delusions.

Dig for the voice that is both not yours and most truly yours.

Only if you are empty enough will you hear it.

20 July

On surveying the accumulation of *stuff*:
Clear the clutter.
Too much comes in.
Too much is ingested.
Not enough time has been given for digestion.
Refuse to let the media intrude.
Too much silt has been deposited.
It is choking the life out of you.
Make sure more goes out of your home than comes into it.

21 July

What expression?
Smug satisfaction that feels superior?
Happy smile that is self-absorbed?
Etched joy that embraces all – and is near neighbour to prayer?

22 July

We seek to help others from many motives – genuine compassion, guilt about an easy life, a need to be liked.

Each counsellor needs reminding of the saying, I'll give you all the help I need.

Be realistic.

Set boundaries.

Keep time alone against all intrusion – even when it makes you feel lonely.

Keep time to focus on the One beyond all.

Glib assurances that you are always available are dangerous and arrogant, conveying the false impression that you are more caring than you are – or can be.

When you are engaged with whoever or whatever, you are not available for anyone or anything else.

When there is nothing in the diary, you may be wise to choose to play – even if you have no partner or children to bring you down to earth.

And in any case you have to sleep and eat.

Of course you are always available for matters of life and death.

But genuine emergencies are few and far between.

23 July

You imagine your 'attachment' is selfless.

But attachment always lays a demand on the other.

Only 'detachment' is free of such burdens.

The task is to be detached not because you are indifferent, but because you love.

24 July

If you put yourself before the Work (the Art, the Composition), neither you nor it will come to any lasting thing.

If you put the Work before yourself, both will endure, though the 'enduring' will of course be hard.

The Work will take you towards what you will become.

It is the servant of your maturing.

25 July

Your voice is singular, particular to you.
But it is the Music that sounds through you.

26 July

To the degree that you are different, so are you special and exceptional.

You have been created with particular care.

And the world has need of you – though the world may ignore you and refuse to listen.

27 July

There is no room for anything but this moment – like the moment of a total eclipse of the sun.

If you miss it, you have lost it.

28 July

The deeper your work, the fewer will be your contacts, 'in-touch-with' you, either other people or words or materials.

A profound resonance is possible only with a few, and this limitation inevitably takes you into silence and solitude.

29 July

Do you 'act' or 'play-act'?

What, for you, is 'all or nothing'?

30 July

Your 'birth' places, or 're-birth' places, or 'death and new birth' places, need calm, boundaries, protection, with no deadlines or hurry.

Such places, 'set apart', radiate energy, affecting other places far distant.

They have to be 'special', excluding none who seek sincerely what they can give, but exclusive in that they have to protect their special purpose, not because of élitism but because of the nature of their task.

And those who guard and serve such places may be 'set apart' too (though never 'separate' and 'above').

[After Janet Baker.]

31 July

Ask of the militants, 'Who has the best songs?'
 Birds of prey foul their nests and sing no songs.

1 August

Give to each other a listening heart, gladly obedient
to the as yet unknown future which will emerge
between you, and which will change you both and
help you grow.

2 August

Your sexual energy can be wasted or it can turn in
on itself.
 Or it can fuel something else that matters more
than release and pleasure, more even than the sustaining of a human love, a deeper and more lasting
creativity.
 It is not usually discovered until the flames glow
and no longer sparkle.
 Some discover it after the age of childbearing,
though the childless of whatever sexual orientation
may discover it sooner.
 How can my sexual energy fuel your uniqueness,
and how can yours fuel mine?

3 August

The Work will defeat you constantly, because it is always greater than you.

You will never really be 'up to it'.

But from such defeats you learn and grow.

4 August

You are drawn to your vocation by mixed motives, including a myriad desires and unmet needs.

Some of those desires and needs will be met, some not.

When you bump against your limits, you will cry out from the emptiness that is un(ful)filled.

That is the moment to *warm* to the impossible.

The rueful wonder will dawn on you that it is precisely from what you find impossible that you will free others to live what you cannot.

This is never easy, but once the way is accepted, your sacrifice will give life to others, and your own impossibilities will lose their bitterness.

Your pain will become so mingled with joy that it loses the name of pain and becomes blessedness.

5 *August*

On objects accumulated, especially on what you 'collect':

Are they any longer practically useful or spiritually nourishing?

If not, sell them, give them away, or dump them.

6 *August*

Simplicity – less clutter.

Silence – less chatter.

Solitude – less matter.

But the things, words, and people that remain really do *matter*.

7 *August*

Outer emptiness brings home inner emptiness, the space that usually needs to be cleared of clutter, chatter, matter, where at last you engage in the most significant struggle, where the pain of loneliness is recognized and lived into, where the implacable and inescapable Thus-ness of Love is encountered.

8 August

If you are fully aware, clear within, open to others, if you are intimately at one with the Source of being, if you are totally free of entanglements, your simple presence, your few words, your accurate touch, will transmit life and will liberate.

[So John V. Taylor understood the presence of Jesus.]

9 August

If my life is not entangled in your pain, I can absorb that pain, swallow it, without its poisoning me.

I will be drained, but not harmed, spent, but ready to be re-charged.

The energy that I need will flow into me as readily as the tide after the ebb.

I receive and ground your pain.

You receive and are lifted by my hope.

Both of us exchange life and touch joy.

In the same way you – or someone else in the great web of being – can receive my pain.

Such freedom however is rare, and usually only partial.

Nevertheless, it is what we seek, and it is what we

are drawn to, in and by the Totally Free Spirit, Whole, Holy Spirit.

(And thus *works* forgiveness: absorbing the offence without throwing back hostility.)

What makes it so hard is that we are rarely free of the entanglement of one another's pain and hurt.

So, together, we need the presence of the One who is pure, unbounded Love.

10 August

On burning boats:

Until you leave behind a chapter of your life, with no way of return, you are still hesitating, you can still draw back; consequently, your energy will be scattered, not focused.

When you do let go, 'Providence' also moves, moves towards you with gifts.

'Events' begin to 'happen'.

Encounters surprise you with what you need.

Material assistance comes to you unexpectedly.

None of these things could you have 'dreamed up'.

You can never be aware of what is waiting for you at the right moment.

11 August

Magnanimity:
  Magna – 'great', *animity* – 'soul'-edness.
Magnanimity:
  'great-hearted generosity'.

12 August

Meditate:
  Medi – 'centre', *tate* – 'stand in the'.
Meditate:
  'stand in the centre'.

13 August

Go deep enough into *anything* and eventually you will become aware that all of it has been shot through with the Divine Presence.

14 August

If you exercise power, make a fool of yourself, and so make others laugh.

15 August

'Come out' as your true self:

You will save your true self from imprisonment and suicidal despair.

You will be at peace, and full of quiet energy, no longer torn between self-hatred and foul temper.

You will be empowered, because you are no longer 'prey' to the lies on which the traps of oppression are constructed.

16 August

You can never *solve* fundamental problems.

They are not 'soluble', they do not 'dis-solve' in water.

They can only be outgrown.

[After Carl Jung.]

17 August

Are those with whom you network part of a burgeoning earth-saving community, or merely a spiritual and material élite?

It is the old question put to ancient Israel:

Are you chosen for privilege and power or for universal service?

18 August

At times of crisis, energy is withdrawn from the hands and feet to keep the core alive.

At such a time you cannot move in the old familiar ways.

The surface streams have run dry, the flow is hidden, underground.

That has been happening to the forms of faith.

And it is necessary, for the time is becoming ripe for new forms to be born.

But for the present, the energy, the water, is hidden, slowly amassing for a new day.

[After Laurens van der Post.]

19 August

Listen for a living word, for *now*, for *today*, a word that simply comes, not thought out carefully beforehand.

We need words that will fall into place, their sequence utterly new, fresh delivered, connected with that ever-present and ever-elusive world of infinite meaning, which is for ever seeking to be articulated by larynx and tongue, teeth and lips, caught on today's new breath.

[After Laurens van der Post.]

20 August

Socrates once said that what was wrong with Greece was that there were too many books.

21 August

From blue jeans to blue rinse the desire to conform is ancient and dangerous.

We have experienced a century of mass conformity in the politics of fascism and communism.

As in a mirror, cancers reflect that history in the human body.

Identical cells multiply at the expense of varied cells, eventually taking over and destroying the whole.

And how much monoculture can replace bio-diversity before the consequence is a desert?

Of course we do not like being warned, even less to act at cost to ourselves.

22 August

Treat your problem as your problem *child*.

Do not commit infanticide.

Reverence your child, however problematic.

Loved and cherished, even in time quietened, your child will lead you to your own deep true being, will take up residence in your heart, and you will find that you have been *enlarged*.

[After Laurens van der Post.]

23 August

Laurens van der Post tells how the Bushmen of the Kalahari Desert would mark their crossing of a river by putting down a stone in honour of their god.

Everybody who came by added a further stone.

The people have now vanished, the piles of stones remain.

We mark significant moments and places with something that has no monetary value, to which everybody can contribute, however destitute.

Mutely, it tells our descendants that we have been this way, and we have left behind us markers that both warn and encourage, that point to a path through dangerous territory, or to those occasions of significance in our lives when something of great meaning has been revealed to us.

Though the revelation for which you look will not happen to you precisely here, be expectant that it will happen, and be encouraged by these signs of encounter and meaning.

24 August

A Bushman once told this to Laurens van der Post.

When sorrow finds a name and a voice, it is like the lightning you see calling and the thunder speaking after it to say that soon the rains will fall on your again.

25 August

Do you in-gest too much, di-gest too little, and gest-ate hardly at all?

Bring probing mind and loving heart, and, above all, imagination to bear on what you take in.

You will then use up the energy it has given you without its turning sour within, so turning on you and eating you up.

26 August

You will convert others not by *demanding* something impossible but by *being* something irresistible.

[After May Sarton.]

27 August

When old ways and structures collapse, religious and political fanatics come out of the woodwork, in fury and hatred, seizing on violent words and weapons.

At such times, who and what are in danger of being swept away by the onslaught?

Careful thought.

Mixed race.

Artistic imagination.

Tenderness.

Cherished land and buildings.

Those lawkeepers and peacemakers who still serve the common good, opposing the lawbreakers and warmongers, those with money and weapons unrestrained, markets rampant and arms traders exultant.

All who vitally protect the boundaries and privacies which value and nurture all that is in danger.

[After May Sarton.]

28 August

When you remember those who have died before you, ask them to make love more wholeheartedly than they ever did in this life, so that their love-making, now more true and accurate and engodded, may overflow to our good.

Is not 'making love', in whatever mode, what is meant by our being partners with 'God' in creating?

29 August

Are you still capable of being pulled out of orbit by violent sudden attraction?

How far are you able to enjoy without needing to possess?

[After May Sarton.]

30 August

Carry through the thrust of energy and rise to meet it, but at the right moment.

Let there neither be premature spurt or yearning, nor withdrawal or collapse.

Let build.

Follow through, and, at the ripe moment, let go.

31 August

You will not find yourself by looking in a mirror, or by hunting some elusive 'self', but by contemplating what is, and by accepting a discipline and routine which keeps you engaged with what is.

1 September

Montaigne reckoned there were four advantages of a poor memory:

    You can't be a good liar.

    You can't tell long stories.

    You forget offences.

    You enjoy places and books a second time round.

    (I think I once heard of a fifth, but I've forgotten it…)

2 September

A friend is one to whom you can pour out all the contents of your heart, grain and chaff together, knowing that the gentlest of hands will take it and sift it, keep what is worth keeping, and with the breath of kindness blow the rest away.

[Arabian proverb.]

3 September

'Friendship is the inexpressible comfort of feeling safe with a person, having neither to weigh nor measure words.'

[Jeremy Taylor.]

❖

4 September

Buildings and representatives of organizations express power, and the power of an organization is greater than the sum of its parts.

It hides the personal truths, weaknesses, and insecurities that are beneath.

Until these realities are expressed, given shape, lived, the rituals of that organization are but hot air, empty balloons.

❖

5 September

If you are a friend of mine, will you be a nettle in my side rather than my echo?

[After R.W. Emerson.]

6 September

If I give myself utterly to you, I put myself in your power, in your grip, at your mercy.

I am at my most vulnerable.

I can but trust myself to your mercies without in advance knowing whether or not they will be tender mercies.

7 September

You are weighed down when you are miserable.

You jump for joy when you receive good news.

That is why you are more afraid of joy than of grief.

For when you jump in the air, you may find you have been swept off your feet.

You may well wonder if many waters might indeed quench love and the floods drown it.

[After The Song of Songs.]

8 September

Movements across: trans-port, trans-fer, trans-form, trans-figure.

We are agents of such movement, such change of place and of shape.

When we are challenged to give up some comfort or security or worldly wealth or position, we prefer others to change rather than ourselves.

Rather than be 'trans-formed' we 'trans-fer' unwelcome change on to others.

9 September

You have a knotty problem to solve (or re-solve)?

Be gently firm enough, enduringly patient enough, quietly wise enough, to stay with the problem 'not knowing' the solution.

Only thus can an answer be given, always other than what you expect.

You cannot solve it by means of what you already know.

You wait upon the gift of something new.

(And you have to 're-solve' if the first 'solution' was premature.)

10 September

You are called not to 'know yourself', but to 'reveal yourself'.

You cannot know yourself on your own: it is only by revealing yourself to another that the truth emerges, for the deepest truth involves the challenges of love.

And that frightens us and requires of us courage and risk.

11 September

Immature virginity is a state of dependence and inconsequence.

Mature virginity is a state of continuing openness, a willingness to greet whoever and whatever calls, to be impregnated whenever and wherever the 'other' draws close.

To be 'ever virgin' is always to be on the threshold, open to the divine exploration, to become an explorer of virgin territory, and an embodier of the Unknown, of the Mystery.

12 September

Take your characteristic stance on the threshold, committed to that which is coming to be.

Make your true home there, so as to be ready to welcome others when they approach their thresholds, and to help them go through and beyond.

13 September

Your beautiful wilderness, vulnerable to intrusion, your creative child self, needs your adult care and your parenting boundaries, so that you can say No firmly to those who would drain you of energy to serve their own demanding and unquenchable needs.

Do not remain swingingly open – as dangerous as being rustily closed – desperately asking for the affirmation that cannot come from the one who is also seeking just as desperately.

You will collude to mutual destruction.

Discern when to be open and when to be closed.

Discern the ones who can give you something when you have stopped demanding everything.

Discern what you need, be clear, then *ask*.

14 September

Are your actions sporadic, dis-connected, momentary, inconsequential?

Or are they repeated, connected, enduring, effective?

Are you *base*-less or well-*grounded*?

Are you existing fatally or living fate-fully?

15 September

Do not hate yourself and destroy yourself.

Love yourself and nourish yourself.

Reverence the Self that is coming to be, taking shape from deep within.

Only then can you reverence others and all creation.

[After Sogyal Rinpoche.]

16 September

Only by exploring the power of your needs will you come to see, temper, and enjoy the power and attractiveness you have for others.

17 September

Do not be afraid of the ebb tide.

Do not resent being becalmed.

Welcome the longer nights as autumn falls.

It is the time of rest, of replenishment.

However bleak, drear, and grey, accept that such a time must be, a day, a week, a month.

Be gentle with yourself.

Any energy you now force yourself to expend will serve only to bring about a collapse when you least want it or expect it.

18 September

Imagine the most compassionate face you have ever seen.

Look at that face, silently, without expectation.

Take that image to yourself.

Imagine your own face to be one with the face of compassion.

Then imagine that compassion flowing to others.

This is prayer.

Then *act* kindly.

So the Compassionate One will live through you.

19 September

If your way is the way of solitude, it will be creative only if it is a way of love, warm and connected, not cold and isolated.

It is a positively sexual way, in a world of bodies, touching matter, loving the world, not with possession, but with compassion.

20 September

To be, as the old hymn has it, 'hidden in thy wounded side', is to be close, very near, absorbing the throbbing of heartlove, the pulsing of lifeblood, the spreading ecstasy of the loins.

21 September

The Alexander Technique is based on three simple 'instructions':
    Let the neck be free.
    Let the back widen and lengthen.
    Let the head go forward and up.
    These are instructions that are thought but not

acted upon, mental pictures that are imagined but
not forced physically.

You simply have to let the physical body do its
own reorganizing.

It is all about being more present, more in har-
mony, more alive.

It is not a million miles from the abundant life of
which the Gospels speak.

22 September

Keep your sense of direction (geographical) and
your sense of direction (spiritual).

Have a sense of line, of alignment.

Keep your eyes on the goal.

Then you will not stray.

The joke is that sometimes you will be so rigidly
aware of the goal ahead that you miss something
vital at your feet.

There may also be an important turning and
your eyes miss the signpost.

Oracles are always ambivalent.

What is nourishment to one person may be poison to another.

What is nourishment at one stage of life may be
poison at another.

23 September

Keep the goal quietly in view: non-possessive love for others, for another; giving and receiving delight and pleasure; creating varied and complex phenomena; imagining the hospitable love of the Three-in-One (which is richer and deeper and more *sexual* than human love, though including that human loving, as well as enfolding the pain of love's absence).

24 September

Is a commitment a confinement or a refinement?
    Purification is a process which burns dross (self) and brightens flames (self-giving).

[After Sr Madeleine.]

25 September

Alone, without relatedness, you atrophy and die.
    Related, without solitude, you suffocate enslaved.

26 September

Resist the temptation to curse the world for pain and death.

Take an impossible hope for your guiding star, stretch yourself to the measure of the distance.

You will then know what it means to live the prayer that we may in the end be delivered completely from the grip of evil.

[After Sr Madeleine.]

27 September

Be in touch with others by the slender threads of mail and phone, and, from time to time, of occasions of meeting, in silence and in celebration, in listening to one another and in reflection, in the spirit of friendship which says:

I need you in order to become myself, to find direction from the cairns you have shaped and placed along the way, to prevent my aloneness from slipping out of creative solitude into an embittered and crabby loneliness, to serve you and be served by you, to vibrate in a tender and intimate touch, and so to share in sacraments of the Living Mystery.

28 September

Your sense of body and place – including churches
– dense, pea-soupy, dark, thick grey, entrapping,
compulsively skewed, or solid, dancing, light, multi-
coloured, freeing, calmly centred.

29 September

When you are challenged by a question you cannot
answer, which makes you feel uncomfortable, especially from someone you believe to be more powerful than you are, or in authority in relation to your
public role, do not do what you *think* they want, and
give an answer to earn approval or deflect criticism.

They are concerned for all those in their sight,
for their well-being, and they do not expect you to
get everything *right*, all the time.

They are challenging you to have courage, they
are willing to explore the questions with you, and
they are refusing to let you escape from what is
difficult, and what, if lived with, can be a point of
growth.

Of course you have to trust your questioners,
having discerned whether or not they are worthy of
that trust.

30 September

Heart-rending…
Heart-embracing…
Heartfelt…
Whole-hearted…
Light-hearted…
Enheartened…
For love's sake…

1 October

Scent the track of the 'God' who has disappeared
over the horizon.

2 October

Listen for the Dream, the Story, the Coming, that
will match the needs of our desperate day.
    All our stories are in tatters now.

3 October

Provisional law says, Your best will be loved; your worst will be judged.

    Necessary gospel says, Your best will be judged; your worst will be loved.

4 October

If anyone sings your praises ask what went wrong with the lyric or the tune, or both.

5 October

Gather.
Listen.
Scribble.
Wait.
Hear.
Write.
Wait.
Detached, *look* at what you have written.
Where did all *that* come from?
You are astonished.
It 'fell in'.
It demands obedience.

6 October

What gets in the way of intimacy?

The terror of being touched accurately and tenderly; the fear of alien touch; the faded memory of possessive or wounding touch.

But if you have seized up, you cannot change.

And if you cannot change, you will not be *alive*.

And you cannot know love.

[After James Baldwin.]

7 October

Be still.
Be silent.
Be the person you wish to be.
Allow space around your 'character'.
Mime.
Dance.
Mime can express tragedy and transformation.
Dance can take both into joy.

8 October

To 'establish' a 'momentum' is to keep a tradition moving.

It is not to set it in stone, in an 'establishment', past its span of life.

All 'establishments' are provisional, for the time being, though no establishments like to recognize that fact.

Like photographs they catch a 'moment' in time, and soon fade.

9 October

According to Thomas Aquinas, 'sin' is that which darkens the mind.

Such darkening refuses to recognize the 'blindingly' obvious.

You are seized by moral blindness, in which state you walk unaware into danger.

Your judgment and your actions become perverse.

Thus you – whether person or community – are 'caught' and 'held' in evil's grip, trap, snare, glare.

❖

10 October

If you dig deep, reflect long, act in spiralling patterns of faithful loving, you will be a traditional radical, continually radicalizing the tradition.

11 October

From time to time face the challenge that comes when cherished ways no longer give you life: Latin Mass, Choral Evensong, Revival Meeting, Alpha Courses, Parish Communion, Midnight Mass, Evangelical Preaching, House Groups, Contemplative Prayer, Meditation Technique.

Let go into a new deep end.

Be stripped of what you once held dear.

Enter a trackless waste, a formless mess, such as is always 'in the beginning'.

And let the Spirit, as always, brood.

One day that will include your disintegrating flesh and blood, your decaying corpse, your bleached bones.

Simply trust that again and again a dying is a prelude to a new life.

12 October

The more status and wealth you have, the louder they will shout, making such a noise that you will be unable to hear the whispered cries of those from whose fear the status has been granted and from whose labour the wealth has been acquired.

13 October

Realize that you are loved, you are accepted, you are forgiven, you are cherished, you are of infinite worth, and others want to give to you.

For without you, both I and we are deprived of all the ways in which you could enrich our lives.

[After Leo Buscaglia in *The Parsonage*.]

14 October

The more consistently, persistently, thoroughly, courageously, you love, the closer you will come to being harmed by those who cannot bear to be loved.

15 October

Soul-deep, your being rises when faced with the implacable thus-ness of a landscape of air and light, of vast horizons, of height and depth.

16 October

For the evening meal – flowers, candle, a half-bottle of good wine, a carefully set table, and one of these – either music or a good book, or a companion.

[After May Sarton.]

17 October

If you are not really with me you are an empty presence.
   If you are fully alive you are a real presence.
   And when you have left, you are still here.

18 October

Be professional for others' sake.
Be amateur (a lover of the work) for your own sake.
Be both, for God's sake.

19 October

Use sternness to ward off distractions.

Use tenderness to evoke truth.

The shaping any creative pulse of energy demands of you a delicate touch and a keeping at bay of the tramplers.

20 October

You are used to living in your own home, with post delivered and access to a phone?

Put your goods in store.

Live for a while remote from telephones (and of course leave your mobile behind).

Do it during a postal strike.

In what ways are you more independent?

In what ways are you more dependent?

21 October

If you are, at least some of the time, *good*, you have doubtless willed it and practised it.

And you will feel superior to those whom you perceive as bad – or at least not as good as you are.

If you want to be *holy*, you will have to admit that you could, under certain pressures, be as bad as anybody else.

And if you do become holy, you will never notice it and be surprised if others say it of you.

Holiness creeps up on you unawares as a gift.

22 October

Sometimes, being alone with the Mysterious One is like a love affair with someone who is very jealous, who is uncompromising, and who gives you nothing that you want.

Only in retrospect, usually years later, do you have a hunch that you have been loved well and to your greater good.

23 October

You are not an individual but a person.

You are not a replaceable spare part.

You may not be indispensable, but you are irre-placeable.

You are singular, unique, unrepeatable.

And everyone and everything is present in you.

You discover who you are only in and through others, in exchange, in encounter, in the to and fro of giving and receiving, in co-inherence.

24 October

Tuck away your faith in the corners of your life, so hidden that you seem to lose it.

But it will still be present in everything that you do.

And if you do speak of it, better whisper than shout.

25 October

Without distinctions you cannot connect.
Without closeness you cannot scrutinize.

[After John Berger.]

26 October

When you cannot avoid living alone, by vocation or more usually by circumstance, rarely by the deliberate choice that, for the recluse, barely disguises a dislike of human beings, you may come to realize that, even if nobody else is there with you, nevertheless you consecrate bread by reverencing it, by expressing gratitude for it, by receiving it as an embodiment of Real Presence.

And you can do this without presbyter or congregation or permission.

You bear in your own being all that is necessary for the evoking and receiving of the Mysterious One.

You are a church in miniature, a micro-church, a cell of the living organism, in communion with all the others, even when awareness slips.

From time to time you need others to avoid being too ec-centric, too off-centre, to be encouraged, to be equipped, and you need others in order to recognize that you belong to a greater whole, more than the sum of all of us.

And you can't celebrate and enjoy a party on your own.

❖

27 October

'Religion' is practised by those who are afraid of hell.

'Spirituality' is practised by those who know what hell is like.

28 October

In the hidden place, in the secret place, you are given a revelation, and from that place you bring it and uncover it.

In the place of burial, of disintegration, there is either nothing at all, or nothing of significance, yet in it and through it there may also be a revelation, the impossible, unexpected gift of resurrection, to be brought out and uncovered.

29 October

A yawning gap (both as in 'wide' and as in 'boring') opened up between pulpit and pew, and into the consequent grave all the abused and murdered words have been thrown.

30 October

What new tune is becoming familiar to your ears, and can you write the words?

What new words are insisting on their presence, and can you set them to music?

31 October

To be completely at rest is to be a corpse, though it may not give you ease to think about it.

Be thankful that you are restless and incomplete.

Being disturbed and imperfect shows that you are still being worked on, accepted by divine grace, and encouraged by divine invitation.

1 November

Nicholas Berdyaev said that we are looking for a new type of saint, for men and women who will take upon themselves the burden of the complex world.

2 November

Prayer is both an awareness of the intolerable and a container for the work of transforming the intolerable.

3 November

Dis-connected, your 'over-powerful' masculine pushes and tramples, like a 'bull elephant'.

Your 'weakened' masculine complains and is inept, like a fluttering 'budgerigar'.

Your 'over-powerful' feminine pulls and devours, like a 'lioness' with her prey.

Your 'weakened' feminine twitters ineffectively, like a lost 'skylark'.

Reconciled masculine is gently strong, a 'dolphin'.

Reconciled feminine is strongly gentle, a 'gazelle'.

The dolphin and the gazelle play together.

A child leads them.

A unicorn smiles on them.

4 November

Do you suffer from the 'haunting' music of a fast-disappearing 'God'?

Are you fearful of the silence that descends?

Can you wait, trusting that new music will begin to be heard?

5 November

Solitary, yet delving the heart of the world and the hearts of human beings, listen, in your inner emptiness, to the profound and neglected language which is indeed 'at the heart' of it all.

The language of truth at its most profound comes from silence at its most profound.

6 November

If, in the house of your life, your pain is the rubble that the builders have left, can you bear the task of creating a garden out of that waste land?

7 *November*

You (or your institutions) are decadent when you try
to maintain, 'at great expense and great incon-
venience old traditions from which the meaning has
departed'.

[Tom Baker.]

8 *November*

You are feeling homeless 'at home', ill at ease within
an institution, hemmed in by however beautiful a
garden.

For any number of good reasons you may have
no choice about staying, but beware of turning in
on yourself.

The alternative is to 'leave home', and in a
wilderness to 'make yourself at home'.

9 *November*

Trusting yourself to fall into the Abyss, you are
caught by the Great Bird of the Southern Seas, the
Albatross of God, Spirit-Blown, who takes you,

pain-wracked and exhausted, by the arms, lifting them up and down in the rhythm of wings, until your being is charged with new energy, enabling to pulse and flow again the warmth that has been locked and frozen in your pain.

You take wing.

Your pain is graced with joy.

You join the Spiral Dance of the Flying One.

❖

10 November

Do not become absolutely attached to any one particular form, but love well whatever form you discern as best – or perhaps as simply good enough – for the time being.

[After J. L. Houlden.]

❖

11 November

Your defences, your roles, your possessions, your status, all are facades, at worst totally obscuring your true self, at best caretakers for that soul-deep self, vulnerable, frightened, yearning.

[After John Lee.]

12 November

Unity is not static equilibrium but dynamic balance,
not a single fixed viewpoint but co-inherence at
every level of reality, an ultimate deep connection,
one with another, that is unbroken and unbreak-
able, a connection of everything and everyone with
everything and everyone.

13 November

Not soul vs. body, or spirit vs. flesh, but surface-self
vs. deep-self, superficial-self vs. core-self, false self
vs. true self, smoke-self vs. flame-self.

[The last contrast, after Thomas Merton.]

14 November

Your anger gives you strength to command a
'power' to go.
    Compassion melts the ice of your hatred of that
power.
    Both are warm.
    Both are needed in order to be free.

15 November

You can use the energy of your anger well if it is contained by trust and constructive intent.

But cold and bitter hatred, cold-blooded vengefulness, eats away inside you, sours relationships, and, if it strikes out, it destroys, leaving ashes in the air and in the mouth.

Ask yourself if you are 'harbouring' resentment, giving it safe anchorage.

Do you want to be free of such raw, clinging bitterness?

16 November

When you are in conflict with others, and you want to resolve that conflict without force, each needs to recognize that the concerns of the others are at some level deep and genuine.

Each needs to become aware that underlying our differences is the reality that we belong to one another.

Neither must claim to be absolutely right.

Each has to face the cost of any process of reconciliation, and that cost must be to be shared.

Each has to acknowledge that the resolution of the conflict will lie *beyond* the current positions of all involved.

17 November

When you are faced with a fanatic, be clear and consistent in where you stand.

Point out where the logic of the person's attitude leads.

Keep a sense of humour.

Do not become trapped into giving back in similar kind.

Use anger sparingly (for there is no relationship to contain it), never detached from truth and compassion.

Tell something of your story, enough to show that you are vulnerable, not enough to be trampled on.

Remember that arguments build up opposing strengths, while stories await a response.

Remember that you may not change your opponent, but you may well influence the onlookers.

18 November

To believe is to cherish someone or something.

It comes from the old word *lief*, with its root meaning of 'to hold dear'.

19 November

Authority – a power automatically obeyed or a presence willingly respected?

20 November

The divine is a continuously present active verb rather than a static definitive noun.

To pray is to be in the present presence and to share in a personal action.

21 November

Skin is delicate, sensitive to touch, exquisitely pleasurable, vulnerably painful.

The two most sensitive surfaces of the body can get clap.

(The other is the eye.)

[After Eric Griffith.]

22 November

If you are unworldly in your religion, you are likely
to have more faith in the powers that be than those
who engage with the world with compassion.

23 November

Do not cut knots.
    Patiently disentangle the threads.
    Pay careful attention to complexities and contra-
dictions.
    Contemplate the presently unresolvable.
    Be content with uncertainty, doubt, mystery.
    Only then decide and act.

24 November

Be loyal to what is yet to be.
    Trust what does not yet exist.
    Listen for what has not yet been heard.
    Look for the as yet unformed image in the piece
of wood or lump of rock.

25 *November*

Your colonizing spirit is of wilful imposed and imposing power, a grand imposition.

You never even consider the possibility that the vanquished and humiliated people you now despise are the only ones who can meet your deepest needs.

But of course you refuse to allow yourself to be vulnerable to them.

[After Rowan Williams.]

26 *November*

You may be 'marginalized' and 'stigmatized' in one or other parts of your life, but quite privileged and accepted elsewhere.

To be totally marginalized is to be pushed off the edge, is to be expendable, as homeless, as slave labour, to be a factory 'hand', dismissible at a moment's notice, to be unemployed and longing for work, to have no say in your destiny and no power to effect change.

27 *November*

Steadily draw near affliction, do not turn away, bring at least a tentative touch, seek to lessen pain, keep hope alive in your heart, do not bury your protest or your questions, patiently probe the dense 'matter' which does not yet yield its meaning.

28 *November*

To take off your shoes as you approach the 'holy ground' that is another human being is to remind yourself that the soles of your feet are tender, as is the soul of the one who needs your kindness.

[After Donald Nicholl.]

29 *November*

You are not truly free if you think that freedom means that you can do what you like and impose yourself on others, insinuate yourself slyly, intrude on privacy.

For in your turn you also wish to be free from encroachment and restraint.

'Autonomy' is not proud isolation nor another word for tyranny.

[After Geoffrey Warnock.]

30 November

Do you pay taxes to Caesar or pay attention to Caesar's slave?

The second is more taxing and more rewarding.

[After William McNamara.]

1 December

Stop trying to define 'God'.

You cannot get beyond the language of Mystery.

Mystery is not a puzzle that you can solve but a question that you cannot answer, a reality that you can never control or 'get to the bottom of'.

You can but live into it – and discover that 'it' turns out to be *more* personal than 'personal', a supra-personal reality at the heart of all things, the *ungrund*, the 'under-ground' of your being.

The reality wells up within you, to the surface, in 'its' freedom and to your surprise.

'It' is gift: 'it' has nothing to do with what you do or do not deserve.

St John of the Cross called 'it' *Todo*, the 'All', and used the word *Nada*, 'Nothing', to describe it, 'it'.

2 December

Unsure that you are loved, that, quite simply, you are of worth, you live for others so much that you refuse to acknowledge your own needs, never ask for anything, and miss those who long to give to you and long for you to receive.

Can you not risk being open?

3 December

Neighbour's shopping bag always lighter than own shopping bag.

4 December

To wash up together lightens the load.

It is lighter for the host: a chore shared becomes enjoyable.

It is lighter for the guest: the task is simpler than at home – you don't have to remember where everything belongs, and it is not your responsibility to put everything in its right place.

5 December

From your belly comes your infant self, roaring, sobbing, shrieking.

Trust the power that your adult self now knows, transforming those wounded sounds, now become growling, rumbling, chuckling.

6 December

Because the clock says so, you wake up now, you are fed now.

Light and food flood you, too suddenly, too much.

Banish the alarm clock ('alarm' is an emergency word), eat when you are hungry.

Discover your own rhythms.

Today, take time out of time, let happen, let be.

7 December

If you are totally aware, totally in touch, totally engaged – here, now, today – tomorrow has no power over you, for it does not even exist.

8 December

Fantasy or vision: how can you tell?
   Ask questions:
   Connections?
   Chores?
   Incarnated?
   Bodies?
   Cost?
   Imagination?
   Detail?
   Solid?
   Metaphors?
   Meetings?

9 December

If you find you have no surface energy, you may need to recognize that *reserve* energy has been depleted, as a *reservoir* after a dry summer.

   Go to your sources of renewal.

   Slow down but do not stop and seize up.

   Keep moving, but gently.

   Drink deep.

   Wait for the flow – it will happen again in its own time.

10 December

The verbal magician can create temporary sacred space for truth, compassion, light, meaning, a space protected from the encroaching falsehoods, from cruelty, darkness, disintegration.

But it is dangerous work:

I sat spell-bound.

I was en-chanted.

I was en-tranced.

When does that become power to bewitch, to spread evil?

And what of such power at religious and political rallies?

11 December

Be jolted out of any complacency that you possess the truth, the Word, *against* all others.

Respond rather to the challenge to live the truth, the Word, *towards* communion with all others.

12 December

Beware honorifics, status, pedestals, podiums, eloquence, well-crafted set pieces, beautifully manicured scripts.

Honour the rejected within you and among you, the quietest voice, the shy presence at the back, a story told in stumbling words, new thoughts expressed under the pressure of an unexpected question, muddle and uncertainty.

13 December

When churches and rulers are in alliance you hear talk of the just war.

When churches and rulers are in tension and opposition, and churches are without political power, you hear of non-violence and passive resistance.

14 December

Eckhart's *grunde* – ground, inner core, kernel, seed bed – *both* the earth into which seeds die *and* the potential for growth.

So works and acts the 'God' of Incarnation.

15 December

Think of the difficult people in your life – the parasites, the devourers, the bludgeoners, the complainers, the grating voices, the fluttering, the twittering, the loud.

Tough – they are your sacred guests, jewels hidden in the mud you splatter them with.

16 December

In the darkness you may not be able to see light at the end of the tunnel, but there is a difference between being stuck in that darkness and moving through it.

Learning to find the way by touch? Learning a new language?

Beginning to see what you miss when you are overwhelmed by too much light?

Making the darkness your home, dwelling there, and keeping faith?

17 December

The five wounds of childhood, rejection, betrayal, denial, abuse, abandonment, all appear again in the story of the last week of the life of Jesus.

[After Katherine Tetlow.]

18 December

What are you ingesting? digesting? assimilating? eliminating?

19 December

'La Belle Dame Sans Merci' is beautiful but cold: a winter sunshine.

No mercy, no *merci*, no thanks, no gratitude; no 'merc-hant', no 'com-merce', no capacity for the kind of exchange by which both parties benefit.

Fathered without tenderness, she is rigid, frozen, and transmits a deep fear to her offspring, spiritual or physical.

Petrified, her flesh has become stone.

Power alone is left to her, eyes as shafts of burning light, ambitious, seeking the wealth and status that keep terror at bay.

20 *December*

Total concentration:

Only the goal matters; grim expression; tight, taut; competitive.

Or: relaxed, focused awareness; waiting for a gift; engaged in a creative task; enjoyment of each moment.

21 *December*

A small pilgrim place: a place of significance (history, beauty, persons), sustenance (spirited and nourishing), souvenir (sacramental keepsake, to bring to mind the occasion when it has gone from the surface memory: 'souvenir', from the Latin *sub-venire*, 'to come from underneath').

In the encounters that may happen, such a place may also be one of sobbing (circles of lament), stories (radical confessional), silence (listening for wisdom), struggle (re-charging the energy in the midst of inner struggle and towards outer struggle).

In the Bible those four aspects are found in Psalms, History, Wisdom, Prophets.

22 December

Jesus – Shame and dishonour;

Early Church – Jesus buried in a rich man's tomb, now seated at God's right hand.

Jesus – Applauds enemies (Samaritan, Centurion) and puts family second;

Early Church – We are law-abiding and no threat to the Emperor; the Jews killed Jesus.

Jesus – Become nobodies, like expendable slave women.

Early Church – Hierarchies of power and control, eventually sitting down with the Emperor.

23 December

Do not be confused: elaborate when necessary, but be lucid.

Do not be complicated: honour complexity but be clear.

Do not be opaque: be as profound as you need to be, but be simple.

24 December

Glory to 'God' in the highest,
and peace to 'God's' people on earth.

Glory to 'God' in the lowest –
peace for all people, shalom for the earth.

25 December

An infant image: a sculpture of a Mother and Child, mother smiling contentedly, child on her lap chuckling.

(Why is so much art with religious subjects so *solemn?*)

Another image: a baby, eyes closed, serene; eyes open, with wonder.

Claim the birthright of the twice-newly-born.

Such a Christ-child be born in us today.

26 December

Religious ritual without love is either sentimental nostalgia or cruel legalism.

Sexual ritual without love is either sentimentality and falsehood or cruelty and meaninglessness.

27 December

Write your own Gospel, not least in your own body, but always as 'updated good news'.

Project on to Jesus the best self you would like to be, the Jesus who has become for those who will pay attention to him, and engage with him, an icon of possibility, for he gave all away, emptying himself, withdrawing so as to let the Spirit connect us with one another.

There was *nothing left*, the nothing out of which new life is always given, and because of which our 'following' is not slavish imitation but creative originality.

[After Dag Hammarskjøld.]

28 December

What punctuation mark signals your view of the future?

Full stop?
Semi-colon?
Question mark?
Exclamation mark?

29 December

Necessity is that which cannot be changed.

It is near neighbour to compulsion, addiction, habitual sin.

Vocation is the call to transform necessity, to create with raw material, to get it *moving*, with the intention of joy.

If there is so *much* to process, solitude will be *inevitable*.

It is an inner journey that does not sit easily with the crowded continuities of 'marriage', but needs com-panions, fellow bread-breakers, friends, guides.

30 December

As these 'waymarks' have taken their final sequence in preparing them for publication, I have realized that there is no reference to Alan Bennett's wry, accurate, and affectionate humour and compassion. In his talks about his childhood, *Telling Tales*, he mentions the picture of God he imbibed as a child, something like, in W. Empson's phrase, 'an omnipotent ferret'.

31 December

On this day in 1900 Thomas Hardy wrote a poem called 'The Darkling Thrush'. A songbird defied the gloom and desolation of the winter landscape, matched by the poet's inscape, and its song seemed one of trembling hope, of which the bird knew but of which he was unaware…

INDEX OF THEMES

INDEX OF PEOPLE, PLACES & TITLES

OTHER BOOKS BY JIM COTTER

The first three prayer books (with Peter Pelz)
Prayer at Night
Prayer in the Morning
Prayer in the Day

A new unfolding of the Psalms
Through Desert Places
By Stony Paths
Towards the City

Reflections and Prayers at the end of an age
Healing – More or Less

Some perspectives on sexuality and spirituality
Pleasure, Pain, and Passion

Patterns of Christian service
Yes...Minister?

Cartoons at the giving of the Peace (with Stuart Yerrell)
No Thank You I'm 1662

Practising Hospitality
Love Rekindled
Resources for a House Eucharist
Love Re-membered

Soundings from a deep depression
Brainsquall

Cairns for a Journey (the first few)
Dazzling Darkness